Photographic Credits:
Georg Müller 20, 24-27
Balthazar Korab 28, 31-33, 42 (below), 44, 46, 47, 50, 52, 54, 55, 64, 67-71, 75 (above), 78, 79, 88, 91, 93, 94, 95 (below)
Stephen L.Rosen 34, 38, 39, 40, 41
Fiona Spalding-Smith 42 (above), 48, 49
Lenscape Inc. 57
Michael Dersin 58, 61-63, 80, 84, 86
Damian Heinisch 72, 76, 77
Alain Jaramillo 83, 85, 87
Erkan Photography 95 (above)
Kerun Ip 75 (below), 96, 99-104, 107-114, 117-122, 124-130, 133-135

Editorial Director USA
Pierantonio Giacoppo

Chief Editor of Collection
Maurizio Vitta

Publishing Coordinator
Franca Rottola

Graphic design
Studio CREA, Milano

English translation and editing
Martyn J. Anderson

Colour separation
Litofilms Italia, Bergamo

Printing
Poligrafiche Bolis, Bergamo

First published February 1999

Copyright 1999
by l'Arca Edizioni
All rights reserved
Printed in Italy

ISBN 88-7838-031-8

Zeidler Roberts Partnership

Zeidler Roberts Partnership
Ethics and Architecture

Preface by Eberhard H. Zeidler
Introduction by Stefano Pavarini

NA   720.82
749   Z45y
.Z45
A4
1999

Contents

9	The Ethical Dimensions of Architecture *by Eberhard H. Zeidler*
13	Technology with a Human Face *by Stefano Pavarini*
19	Works
20	Cinedom in MediaPark, Cologne, Germany
28	Confederation Life Canadian Head Office, Toronto, Ontario
34	Raymond F. Kravis Centre for the Performing Arts, West Palm Beach, Florida
42	Ford Centre for the Performing Arts, North York, Ontario
50	The Hospital for Sick Children, The Atrium, Toronto, Ontario
58	University of Maryland Medical System, The Homer Gudelsky Building Baltimore, Maryland
64	CIBC Commerce Court Renewal, Toronto, Ontario
72	University of Toronto - Joseph L. Rotman Centre for Management, Toronto, Ontario
80	Columbus Centre of Marine Research and Exploration, Baltimore, Maryland
88	Ontario Cancer Institute Princess Margaret Hospital, Toronto, Ontario
96	Ontario Science Centre - OMNIMAX Cinema and Renovations, North York, Ontario
104	National Trade Centre at Exhibition Place, Toronto, Ontario
114	The Living Arts Centre, Mississauga, Ontario
122	Sunnybrook Health Science Centre - Clinical Services Wing, North York, Ontario
130	431 Glencairn Avenue, Toronto, Ontario
136	List of Works
139	Profile of Firm

The Ethical Dimensions of Architecture
by Eberhard H. Zeidler

Since the beginning of time, we have searched for meaning in the world around us, but this search has proven elusive: no sooner do we make sense of our surroundings, than our ever-inquisitive mind reaches out towards new and unknown fields.

Herein lies architecture's timeless appeal, for in its solid, stable structures we see a world that we can understand. Our built environment reflects not only our need for shelter, but also our innate impulse to wrestle order out of chaos and our striving for a rational, comprehensible world. However, notwithstanding our best efforts, there have always been limits to what we can order or understand. In these moments, we have looked to religion as a means of bridging the gap to that which we cannot fully understand. Our need for order has also been reflected in art. If we look at the paintings of the Romantics, John Constable for example, we see a world that is real, tangible and "beautiful."

But that reality has vanished, and today we have reached a point where we no longer know what reality is. We hypothesize that the world began with the "Big Bang", and we are somewhat certain about the elements which came into being a mini-second after the Bang, but when we attempt to understand the Bang itself, we are humbled by the ever-expanding universe and that which lies beyond. In fact, we have even come to wonder whether there even is a beyond.

Architecture is caught in the same dilemma. We cannot express architecture without first trying to grasp our place in this new world view.

When we study the architecture of the past, we see how each period or style reflected the views of the people at that time. For example, the buildings of the Italian Renaissance are the embodiment of 15th century philosophy, religion and science. As "rational" knowledge increased toward the beginning of the 20th century, it was reasoned that every dimension, except rational thought, would be cast away and that, in time, rational thought would explain everything. The Western world began to advance on a dangerous course, a path where architecture was perceived as a timeless rational art.

When we first adopted this rational-architectural view of the world, we believed that it would bring about a better standard of living; that it would provide us with the means of closing the gap between the rich and the poor; that architecture could divest itself of the seemingly unnecessary ballast of the past; that cities would reorganize themselves into desirable districts for work, living and entertainment; that urban dwellers would bask in the light, enjoy good health and benefit from speedy automobile connections. Yet, at the moment a solution finally seemed within our grasp, the dream began to disintegrate: we began to careen on a frightening course, a world without direction, full of teeming, confused cities with an ever-growing distance between the haves and have-nots.

The time has come to reflect on what has gone wrong and to ask whether there is a way for architects to extricate themselves from this senseless path and contribute to a better world. Architecture, after all, does more than provide shelter for people: it also expresses the social and spiritual dimension of humanity.

In other words, we cannot attempt to deal with architecture unless we include and comprehend life in its fullest sense. Our rational approach to life has kept us from exploring and recognizing other means by which we could understand our existence. The rational approach overemphasizes a rational market economy in which capital is the only acceptable yardstick for measurement. Social capital is therefore neglected, and is only included as a means of improving market capital. Neglecting social capital, which also includes spiritual values, has led to a one-sided economy and has diminished architecture. Unless we reevaluate our approach to life, we will not be able to reconnect with architectural philosophy and we will not be able to bring it back to full bloom.

Let us explore this development in detail.

When Quantum mechanics began to explore the nature of the atom's building blocks, an inconsistency was found in the prevailing paradigm of the positivistic attitude. Entire elements, regardless from which infinitesimal nature they were taken, seemed to have no end, but seemed rather to harken back[1] to relationships with each other that could not be measured with the tools of classical physics. Furthermore, the existence of the wave and the particle depended on the the observer measuring them, something which contradicted the beliefs of classical physics. Einstein could not accept this approach and pronounced that "God would not play dice with the Universe." According to contemporary scientific thought, however, God does. God does not rule outside the Universe as the Scientific Revolution believed, but rather, His spirit permeates the whole system—the main building block of the new understanding.

We can no longer explain the world through the positivistic philosophy that began with Descartes. This philosophy posited that the mind and body were separate entities: it was thought that the mind acted independently of the body. Investigations in Quantum physics and in psychiatry have shown that this is not so. The actions of the mind and body are intrinsically related; both shape our understanding of reality. An apt analogy is that of a magnetic field in which one pole represents the part of the mind (as believed in the Cartesian system) which deals with cognitive and rational issues and the other pole represents the part of the mind which deals with non-cognitive, unconscious issues that are part of the both the mind and the body. These poles cannot be separated as they form one unit.

Let us take a look at this new paradigm in relation to architecture. Modern architecture once believed that beauty was a rational event, and that meaningful beauty was that which could only be explained through rationality. Hannes Meyer summed up this attitude with the dictum: "Function + Construction = Architecture." It was held that architecture that was not based on this formula could not be beautiful and had to be written out of the equation. While one can admire the past, the past no longer applies; periods that embraced a repeat of the past, such as the Victorian era, were considered eclectic and "dishonest." This approach has been compared to a modern baseball player who dresses up in a 16th century costume to play the game.

So the sarch for a new model of beauty, based solely on function and construction that would be appropriate for the 20th century, began. However, the forms available to express this model were limited and the question arose as to whether they were valid. In other words, when the function changed, the perfect form became fictitious; when old technologies could be built at the same price, or even cheaper than new ones, and when our emotions longed for something more than rationality, then the new dictum became questionable.

At this time, opposition to the Modern theory, such as Post-Modern architecture, sprang up. However, instead of abandoning the Cartesian paradigm altogether, they merely added another dimension to it - a dimension which was previously felt to be missing in architecture. Oswald Mathias Ungers, in his manifesto, said that function and construction were merely the slaves of the architectural idea, thereby turning the rational credo on its head and making Emotion the only master.

It would be wrong to say that Modern architecture did not create beauty, for it did open a window to the exploration of new technologies, and it did find new solutions to functional requirements and, indeed, beautiful buildings like the Villa Savoie were built. However, the new vocabulary was limited.

A parallel phenomenon took place in some areas of fine art where, reliance on rational principles produced movements like Conceptualism and Minimalism, which, while opening up new vistas, remained restrictive.

The problem with such a linear approach to the creation of architecture and art based on a Positivistic philosophy was obvious, as it is impossible to create architecture or art based on the logic of the spoken word. If this approach could adequately express the desired meaning or result, then it would no longer be necessary to build or paint. As Isadora Duncan said, "If I could tell you what my dancing means, then there would be no point in expressing the idea through dance." It is important to include the emotional and subjective elements which cannot be articulated or rationalized into architecture and into art.

Now let us consider these thoughts as they apply to urban planning.

Visionaries, such as Le Corbusier, thought that the street, the city's main element, was a remnant of the shadowy past when the sun was denied entry into the city and should therefore be eliminated. His vision was not that of a community living together, but that of an individual, perched high on a balcony, who would box away the afternoon in a Hemingwayesque eternal holiday, while glancing from time to time at the vacant green space below.

However, in this city the individual still needed transportation. The segregation of the road system into independent pedestrian pathways, collector roads, or highways, was required to move the individual through this vision of a "city in a park." The result was that people's lives were segregated into living, working, and recreation, and were not integrated as they used to be in the cities of the past.

Modern city planning took these motifs and brought them to a conclusion. The "rational" split of the city into residential, working and entertainment areas led to the development of suburbs, resulting in a lifestyle where the car was a necessity. In turn, this led to the destruction of integrated downtown shopping areas and to the creation of suburban malls and isolated super-warehouses.

Modern city planning also segregated architecture from urban planning. Architects no longer felt it necessary to respond to the genius loci of the city. Rather, it became more important to build an architectural masterpiece, however isolated and glorious, than to dovetail with the surrounding urban texture.

Slowly, planners and architects realized that

further development of the Cartesian paradigms would have a deleterious impact, not only on urban planning and architecture, but also on human behavior. The disruption of the delicate balance of city life is evidenced in the stagnation of human habitats and in the resulting destruction of the human spirit. The Cartesian concept of a mind-body split has had serious consequences that include addictions to alcohol, drugs and even to work. This split is exemplified in the dual ethics of Maxima, or "maximization", which is destructive, and of Optima or "Optimization", which recognizes the limits of cognitive control as the value system of living entities[2].

Accepting this new paradigm of "Optima" may seem like a return to the time prior to Descartes, but in fact it is not, because the rational advances that have been made are still valid and respected. What we need to achieve is the integration of social and emotional issues into the rational approach.

The inclusion of social capital (defined as networking, trust and norms by Robert Putnam) has, at first glance, little to do with market capital, since it does not seem to add monetary value to the equation. However, in the end it is closely related, since without it, market capital will be diminished, deformed or, at worst, will collapse. In the past, religion provided this necessary social capital, but today it can no longer fulfill this role since, in the western world, religion has become too diverse and too weak.

Nevertheless, we still must respect the unconscious demands which, in our time, no longer spring from animistic behavior or from other related actions, but which well up out of the unconscious awareness that is within us all.

It is difficult, if not impossible, to explain this inner self in words. Tacit knowledge can never be rationally expressed, but we do recognize its existence. We know it is there and we can explain some of its aspects. We accept that it is no longer necessary to demote art and philosophy to mere handmaidens of logic and science. The key to this new awareness lies in a balanced, holistic approach integrating art, philosophy and science into an indivisible whole.

We must ask ourselves, however, if such a holistic approach is just another utopian vision, unattainable and with no broad support. Witness our current tendency to pay lip service to ecological concerns through the various popular expressions of a desire to preserve Mother Earth, or through the current proliferation of disparate sects and misguided gurus.

In the end, only two paths remain which could lead to the betterment of humankind: the first is to continue to believe in the Cartesian paradigm with its inherent mind-and-body split and its rational drive (this approach will probably lead to our destruction as a people and to the annihilation of the world as we know it); and the second is to listen to our inner voice (tempered with rational thought) and through such cybernetic control, detach ourselves from this dangerous, unbridled positivistic drive and bring our world, once again, into balance. The question of whether we will be able to achieve this balance in the coming 21st century still remains, but there is no doubt that the Cartesian paradigm is waning and a new paradigm is being shaped.

Today we live in an age completely dominated by a monetary economy, an age in which the cash value of things has become the only value. Money's seemingly unlimited ability to reproduce itself has created the illusion of progress ad infinitum, and time is equated with money. Cognition, reality, and scientific methodology are integrally related to the rise of capitalism. However, in the 21st century our approach to work will change. How this will manifest itself remains to be seen. In this age of constant change it is nearly impossible to assess what is of lasting value, but we can be sure that a new approach will evolve, one that will finally bring about a different environment, one which we can only but glimpse today. This holistic paradigm will embrace value without sacrificing fact.

The new paradigm will not discount scientific intelligence, only the inability of the rational approach to place itself within a larger context from which to observe the world. This new model will enable us, once again, to not only have a career, but to also live a full life, a life in which an enlightened city culture will embrace a holistic architecture enabling us thereby to put an end to the blights of urban sprawl. In this new age, work, spirituality and leisure will dovetail seamlessly, and there will be little interest in profit as a purpose in itself. As Morris Berman said in *The Reenchantment of the World*[3], "The planet simply cannot support the world of an expanding gross national product." We must return, as the I Ching says, and "go down to the very foundations of life."

1) Fritjof Capra, *The Tao of Physics: An Exploration of the Parallels between Modern Physics and Eastern Mysticism*, 3rd ed., updated.

2, 3) Morris Berman, *The Reenchantment of the World*.

Technology with a Human Face
by Stefano Pavarini

The world in which we live seems to have repressed any form of architecture geared to people and their needs. What we mean by this is that architecture has lost that representative role in the collective psyche that used to enable individuals to identify with community buildings. A building's power lay in its ability to turn into a symbolic landmark for a group of people. Nowadays, we are left with an indistinct mass of buildings that have quite literally lowered the standard of public taste. Almost everybody is striving desperately to commercialise forms that destroy any trace of stylistic experimentation.

In the recent past, there was a lot of talk about designer architecture like Aldo Rossi's or Peter Eisenman's cardboard architecture.

This was the era of nostalgia and brainteasing. After the recent wave of deconstructivist architecture, which was all really much the same, we have now entered the age of virtual/digital architecture. A different kind of parallel reality has been constructed in mentalese that has moved beyond deconstruction into the cyberworld of simulation. The basic idea is the same: to create an alternative dimension for design in which everything human or physical has been removed. Personally, I have nothing against the new opportunities offered by modern technology, on the contrary, long live technology! But the impression I get is that the flaunting of technological design is often causing us to lose touch with reality, like the sailor navigating through a virtual rendering of Venice depicted by William Gibson in Idoru.

In contrast, Eb Zeidler's architecture takes us right back to everyday reality with a human face. His real priority is for people living in the kind of ordinary space we all inhabit. The designs pouring in through the media like virtual goods seem basically to have removed any sense of human relations. Or rather the interaction is mediated through money, the kind of relation we have between a buyer and his goods. We have become consumer subjects and objects of desire through the mechanism of simulation, to use Baudrillard's terminology: we are the dream of goods. Modern-day architecture is an integral part of this process of seduction through its new technological gadgets.

But what is left when the flood of images and simulated worlds has run out? In the end, the same old need and desire to live in renovated spaces re-emerges, a longing to experience real architecture whose construction features are capable of embracing the body, mind and spirit.

Nowadays, the kind of alteration brought about by digital simulation offers a kind of psychedelic experience, oneiric interaction with an alternative world which, nonetheless, plunges us back into everyday reality as it always has been, in the discomfort of spaces designed with power and trade rather than people in mind.

In these circumstances, Eb Zeidler's design philosophy and the work of his firm are like a breath of fresh air. His work is inspired by realism or rather reality. This claim should not be taken negatively or with an air of sadness, but as a methodological symptom of attention, a capacity to get involved and an ability, above all, to focus on the real subject of building, which is not architecture but man himself, the city and life that goes on inside it.

All the projects designed by the Zeidler Roberts Partnership outlined here are characterised by the need to interact, to go out, get to know, and truly comprehend the real inhabitants of works of architecture. It is not design, viewed as a means of seduction, that is the real driving force behind his work; neither is it stylistic invention, nor the prophetic announcement of some new trend or other, designed to make the project-product more intriguing. The real centre of attention is architecture as a service, as a means of bringing people together and solving (or at least facing) real situations of everyday life. This does not mean sloppy forms or a return to pauperist-politicised architecture which is a slave to sociologism or some other liberating utopia. Quite the contrary: Zeidler's architecture is deliberately designed to be a form of art applied to reality, operating on a practical level with market demands, costs, building site constraints, the laws of construction, contracts and increasingly low budgets. He works in the dreary reality of business, discerning where the real demand for architecture lies and attempting to meet this demand with artistic building forms. This careful approach has produced fine works of architecture that are pleasant to look at without reverting to the kind of reflexiveness that often focuses more on the designer of a building than on the basic idea underscoring it: we end up pondering over the meaning of the latest design of some star or other of the multi-media system now governing the world of design. Zeidler's world is not the world of Narcissus flattened into his own image, but, if anything, Alice through the looking glass. His methodological pragmatism is geared to definite goals. The real key to a given architectural problem almost inevitably lies in public congregation places, since meeting places are the real focus of design. This is most evident in the huge multi-storey lobbies bearing Zeidler's signature: they physically embody a desire to be covered, coated and sheltered away safely.

Nowadays, lobbies tend to be little more than archetypes of commercial architecture, used as symbols of economic power in most cases or, in any case, the flaunting of a huge waste of meaningless space. Zeidler, on the other hand, uses the emptiness of lobbies to create a symbolic landmark characterising an entire design. The dilation of symbolic space is as important as the concentration of functional spaces.

Turning rationalist dogma on its head, we might call this a sort of existenz-maximum, a quest for fullness opposed to closure and constraint.

This is where Modernism (of which Zeidler is a direct descendent) draws force and inspiration from the world of perception and a certain sensitivity to questions of corporeality and participation. His work is shot through with experimentation into balanced tensions, solids and spaces, density and dilution. As Rosario Assunto has cleverly pointed out, the multiplicity-variety of cities contrasts with the flatness of standard design that "identifies multiples, and multiplies what is identical".

Zeidler's lobbies are the equivalent to the old Greek agorà or public meeting places that turn into the core of his buildings or, perhaps more significantly, the core of the city, while still belonging to his buildings. Zeidler wants his buildings to be fragments of life, bits of the city, and that is what a lobby is. City and building are fused together in a symbiosis in a place where the multitude of people coming together to congregate is not just an indistinct mass, but a sequence of faces and forms that inject life into the space. Interaction between architecture and people is carefully concocted by the architect like an alchemist's potion.

The American metropolis, viewed as a uniform expanse of containers of money-making space geared to speculation, thrives on its capacity to create free architectural structures in the spirit of the pioneers carefully designed with the potential to host human interaction. This is even more striking in someone with a European background like Zeidler, as can be seen, for example, in his hospital facilities, theatres, multi-screen cinema designs and, of course, his scientific entertainment centres.

The lobby of the Hospital for Sick Children in Toronto, Ontario, is carefully designed to restore a sense of dignity to hospitals. Life is injected back into a place were illness is accidentally separated from the body of the city. (We cannot help thinking of the late Giovanni Michelucci who prepared to design in a hospital by spending some time in a hospital amidst the sick to get a real idea of their living conditions).

Zeidler shows that an attractive lobby, amongst other things, helps, at least partly, to create a sense of life, happiness and freedom for children even in a place like a clinic. The brightness and liveliness of an urban plaza help raise the patients' spirits: their suffering is alleviated, at least in psychological terms (which is not to be sneered at). As usual, Zeidler's open spaces are filled with meaning: his lobbies are not just focal points, they also provide the chance for a highly unusual aesthetic experience of great emotional force. They provide a place for holding concerts, playing games, admiring sculptures and meeting together. Children are entranced by what they find in the lobby, without ever losing sight of the fact that they are there to get well again.

The hospital is also designed with the entire administration-medical staff in mind, so that everyone working on the premises feels at home and actively involved in the decision-making processes. This kind of interactive work method makes life easier for the architect, although he does have to pay greater heed to what other people have to say; but this does at least ensure that everybody is happy with the final project. (The same approach has also been used for the Columbus Center in Baltimore, where every single research worker actually signed the blueprints for approval, even the plan for the electrical system!)

The Homer Gudelsky Building and Princess Margaret Hospital are geared to the idea of a hospital-hotel, working around a huge shopping centre-style lobby where the feeling of sadness associated with a clinic is cut at the roots by the happy atmosphere of a place deeply entrenched in urban life. As Zeidler himself points out: "The mind and body are not separate entities and we believe that people recover more quickly in a place where they feel at ease".

Zeidler's desire to create empty/full spaces provides a chance for encounters even in his theatre designs: a sense of theatre is taken into the lobby, where people meet together and actually create their own performances; human interaction and exchange is a show in itself. These spaces are immensely resourceful in gauging our capacity to hold together and encourage community life amidst the alienating effects of the modern metropolis.

Zeidler's anti-conformity is not just skin deep: every single space has a clear sense of its own and must be designed to express this deep meaning, without conceding anything to the latest tendencies and trends. To be classed hi-tech a building does not have to be made out of pipes, cables and lifts visible from the outside. The Cinedom in Cologne's Mediapark has its own thick building skin acting as a tangible form of mediation between the inside of the building and the city in which it stands. Industrial-style design is rejected in favour of something with the force of an idea and a taste of the past as a symbol for the community.

Zeidler is pointing out that technology can be incorporated in a building that looks to the past as a form of narration and not just empty citation.

It is no coincidence that Zeidler has chosen to focus much of his professional career on the most dominant force in contemporary society: the entertainment industry.

Zeidler's project for the Mediapark is designed to be almost a place of worship, a sort of basilica for the secular celebration of representation. His Cinedom, an authentic "dream factory", conjures up the magical spirit of Hollywood in the 1930's as a modern-day myth.

Zeidler's theatrical machinery hinges around a combination of tradition and modernity. He moves in the gaps and folds between the past and present. Traditional forms like the horseshoe-shaped hall are integrated by the latest sound technology.

The Ford Centre for the Performing Arts in North York, Ontario, clearly plays on the huge triple lobby shared by the three different theatres under the same roof. The technical complications that this was bound to cause certainly did not seem to bother Zeidler. Indeed, he has seized this chance to bring together audiences of different kinds, exploiting the "human electricity" generated by this melting pot of social interaction. Zeidler has adopted this anti-elitist approach to construct a "people's theatre". In distinctly European fashion, the entrance lobby is the most important space of all. The lobby mediates between the cityscape and theatrical setting. It provides an introduction to the magic of the stage and an entrance into a different world, the imaginary world of fiction. The lobby area is the place where individuals and groups quite literally inter-act, where a person can find his own personal space in direct contact with the happy troop of spectators who have gathered there for the show. This daring work of architecture puts North York firmly on the map of Canadian culture.

Zeidler's work is shot through with the idea of rendering human interaction spectacular, by which we mean that need for lively communication between people, an open-armed embrace involving the entire community. The spectacle is not just a chance to forget the rigours of everyday life. On the contrary, the show encourages us to study things more carefully and learn: this is the kind of scientific spectacle Zeidler has boldly embarked upon in creating a landmark like the Omnimax Theatre in the Ontario Science Centre, Toronto.

The construction draws on a contradictory combination/juxtaposition of structures. A kind of rampant functionalism designed to stylistically transform the activities performed inside, duly mirrored in the building facade; the exhibition spaces are juxtaposed in complete transparency through a mixture of canvas and glass, while the theatre's metal sphere, an exuberant sign of grandeur, marks the rebirth of a scientific form of representation of great emotional force.

But perhaps the much acclaimed Living Arts Centre in Missisauga is the real height of interaction between building and city. The local community does not just interact and intermingle in the lobby during a break between one performance and the next, people are actually encouraged to get involved in the performances themselves. The centre contains special spaces designed for artistic research and experimentation, where the artists come into direct visual contact with visitors who watch and offer advice as active participants in the work.

The idea, of course, is to inject fresh life and create new emotions in a rather dull urban environment. This even involves revitalising a place bearing such a prestigious architectural signature as Pei's - dating back to the 1970's, a quality design located in a rather lifeless place. Pei's dazzling architectural design for the Canadian Bank of Commerce now finds itself faced with a new shopping plaza that Zeidler has attempted to transform into the kind of place that attracts people's interest rather than driving them away. Changing a rather indifferent space into a different space is the kind of challenge that shows whether architecture is still capable of conjuring up real events at the community's service. Visitors to the CIBC Commerce Court cannot help but think that something extraordinary is going on down here, as they contemplate the building's daring geometric forms.

Human interaction is the real key to Zeidler's carefully balanced designs: scrutinising how man interacts with space and how he hopes to live. The architect must work to give architectural expression to people's desires, observing human behaviour so that "people can do what they want, not what you want", to quote Zeidler himself; this (apparent) platitude totally wipes out that aura of almost God-like privilege associated with architects: take, for instance, all those spaces built during the Modern Movement on the basis of cold standardised calculation in an attempt to harness life inside functional formulas. What the dynamics of behaviour really require are new spaces brimming with excitement; Zeidler's design for the CIBC has brought the power of forms generated by fractal dynamics into interaction with the stillness of Pei's Euclidean immobility. Not out of some sort of stylistic rejection of dull rationalism, but due to a naturally spontaneous desire for change and innovation.

Zeidler has sensed the need to break down the communications barrier between architectural design and ordinary people, who spend hours in shopping centres, theatres, hospitals and other such places. Architecture ought to be able to intrigue ordinary people.

It is no longer a question of choosing between the artist inspired by his/her Muse in some ivory tower or a servile bending to the desires of popular opinion. Both these design approaches lead to useless or even harmful constructions: cold and abstract the former, boring and mediocre the latter.

On the other hand, an architect "after Zeidler's heart" looks, listens and learns from other people's behaviour, striving with each new project to find a new way of serving, surprising, exciting, enticing and inspiring his fellow man.

Works

Cinedom in MediaPark
Cologne, Germany

Cinedom was the first building to be realized within MediaPark, a 50-acre urban redevelopment of former railway lands in downtown Cologne. The urban design for MediaPark was determined as the result of a competition won by Zeidler Roberts in 1989. This private/public sector enterprise will, on completion, contain 1.5 million square feet of media and telecommunications facilities, offices, housing, and a hotel. MediaPark is an innovative urban community embodying new concepts for the integration of commercial, residential and cultural activities. Planners envisioned Cinedom as an anchor of this part of the city, one which would activate the pedestrian life of the main plaza, similar to Piazza del Campo in Siena.

During the first half of this century, movie attendance enjoyed a "Golden Age." However, with the advent of television and home video, as well as the introduction of inferior multiplex theatres, audiences began to dwindle. Cinedom represents a new generation of theatre complex, aiming revive the allure of the movie theatre through architectural statement. Cinedom combines the highest quality of cinematic presentation with the social and communal life that are part of the movie-going experience.

The Rotunda, a 100-foot high glass enclosed entrance hall, serves as the focus of the building's identity. Multi-use activities make it a lively meeting point and marketplace. The hall is encircled on all levels with galleries and lively restaurants, bars, pool halls, and shops. The feeling of urban life and movement is heightened by glass escalators which traverse the Rotunda and connect the various levels. The goal to transform movie-going into a social event where one could see and be seen has been accomplished. A beautiful view opens from the Rotunda onto MediaPark's main plaza and lake. In return, the activities displayed in the Rotunda serve to enliven the pedestrian life of the plaza itself.

Cinedom's thirteen cinemas are located on three levels, the upper two are accessible via the Rotunda's escalators. Between the foyer and the cinemas, the foyer is cut open and connected to each cinema entrance by a bridge, creating a wondrous sense of space. From each cinema bridge you can see the other bridges. In the foyer, the cinema walls are approximately 300-feet long and 60-feet high and filled with huge reproductions of a mural created by Canadian artist, Phil Richards, depicting actors of the past and present "waiting for the show to begin."

Each cinema provides viewers with the optimal film experience. Designed as the fourth wall, a 35-mm Cinemascope screen curves slightly as it fills the entire space and allows for unimpaired views from every seat. State-of-the-art audio is provided by THX sound systems. Complete enjoyment of the film experience is ensured by comfortable seats, which are 26 inches wide, provide 36 inches of leg-room and are set in a steep rake. Cinedom's 13 cinemas provide a total of 3,156 seats and 57 wheelchair spaces. Eleven of the cinemas provide seating for approximately 100 to 300 people. A 700-seat and a 500-seat cinema are available for premiere performances and special movie screenings.

In addition, Cinedom features the "Black Box" performance space which is used primarily for the staging of experimental theatre, film and music productions. It can also accommodate special events such as fashion shows, banquets and seminars. The space is fitted with motorized retractable seating, a telescopic stage, moveable acoustic panels, and advanced lighting and sound systems. It can accommodate a maximum of 372 people with additional space for 10 wheelchairs.

The architectural form of Cinedom employs a playful use of geometric shapes, while following the urban design guidelines prescribed by MediaPark's master plan. The facade is surfaced with sandstone and stucco, which are traditional Cologne construction materials. The design does not reiterate rigid classical symmetry, but rather utilizes varied geometric forms to create a dynamic yet balanced structure. The composition of different forms, and the use of contrasting straight trusses are not merely aesthetic, they play an important role, giving the building its unique character. The decentralized technical areas along the street facade, for example, are enclosed with wave-like walls of glass blocks and are illuminated from within at night. The dramatic glass Rotunda is a spectacular showcase for the building, not only during the day, when its restaurants and cafes are active, but also at night, when the Cinedom is alive with movie-goers.

From bottom of page up, plans of the ground floor, the mezzanine over the ground floor, the upper floor, and the mezzanine over the upper floor.

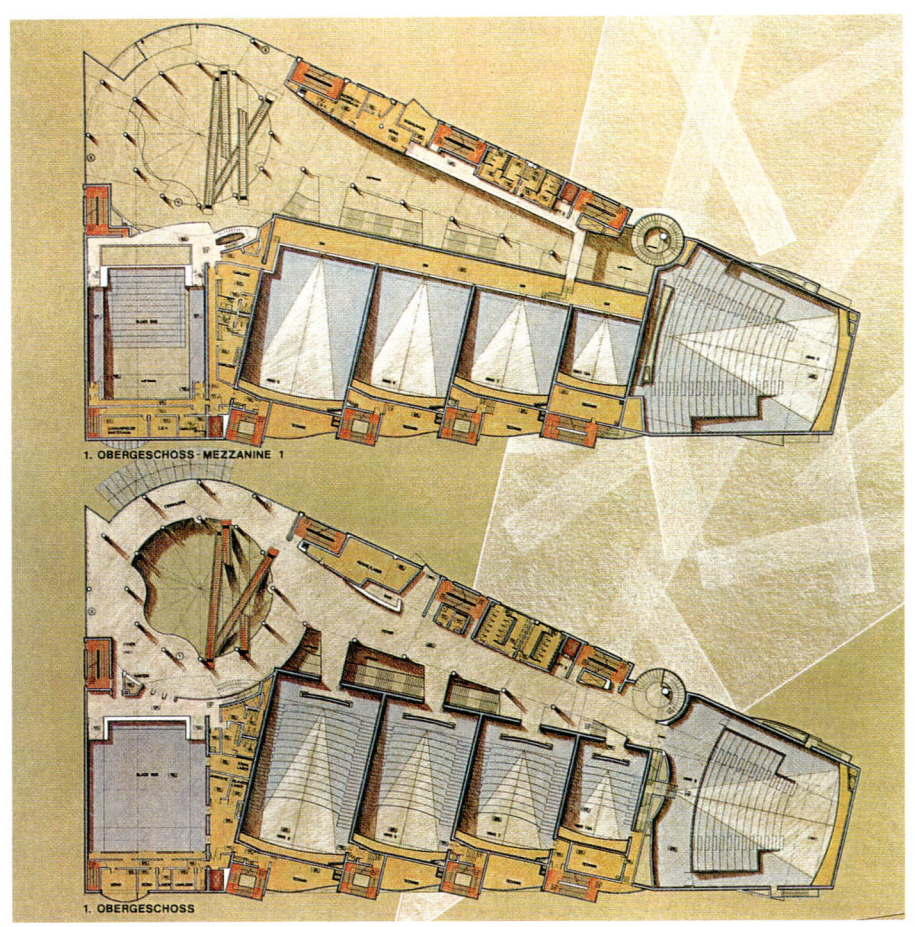

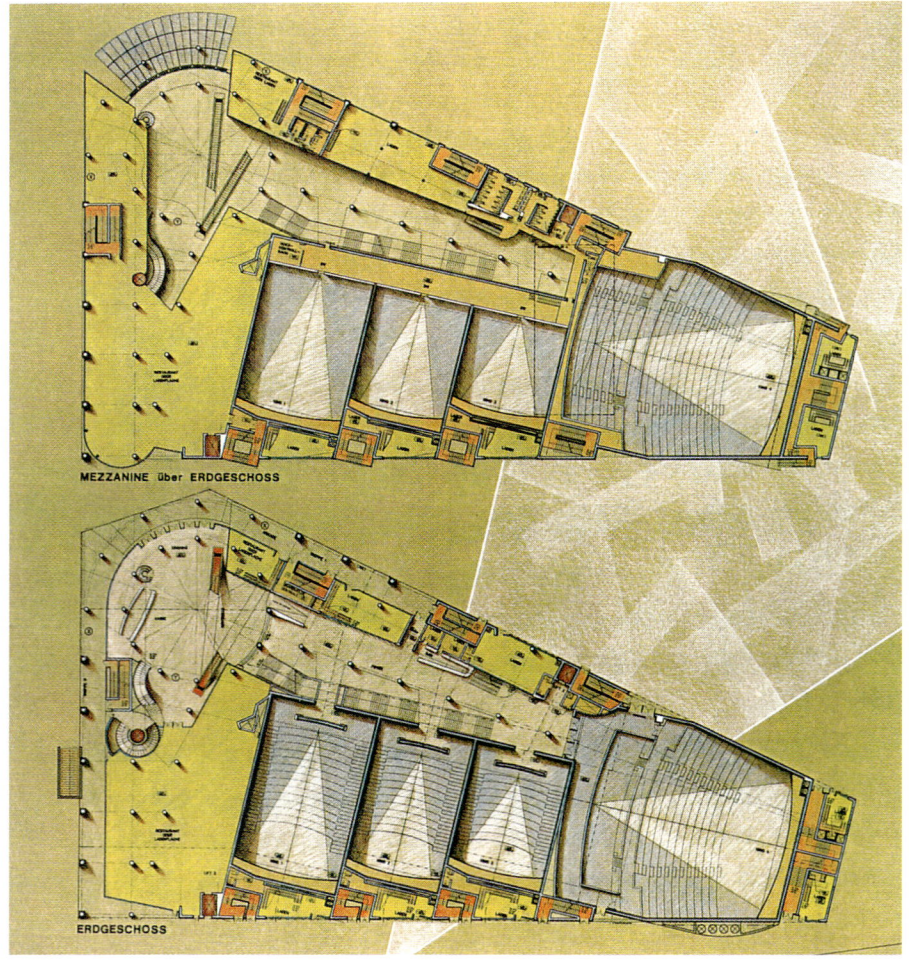

From bottom of page up, longitudinal section, cross sections and view of the model of MediaPark. Urban concept also designed by Zeidler.

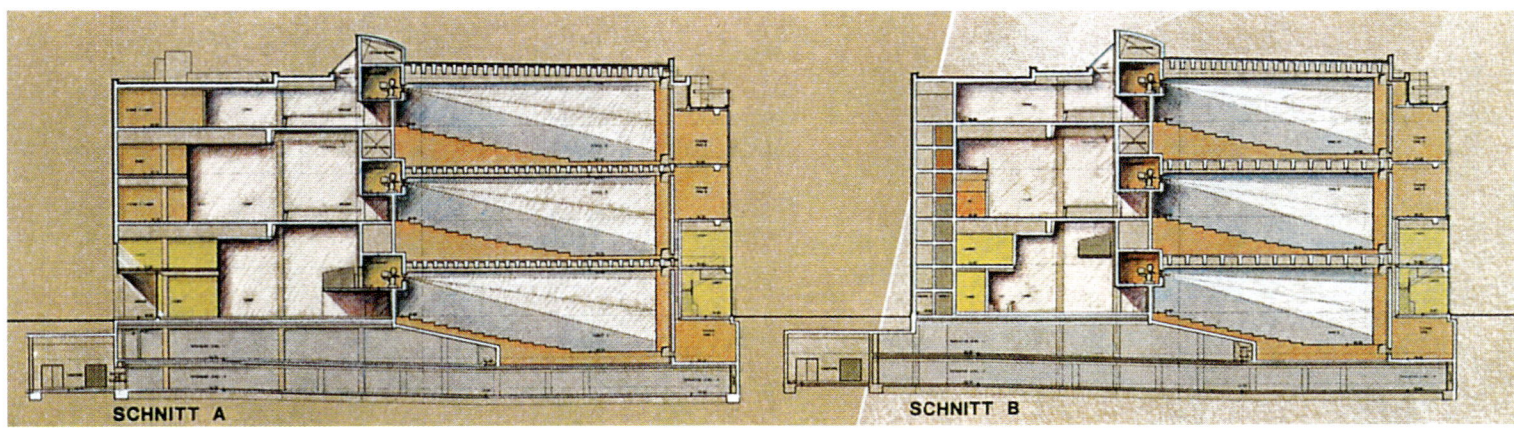

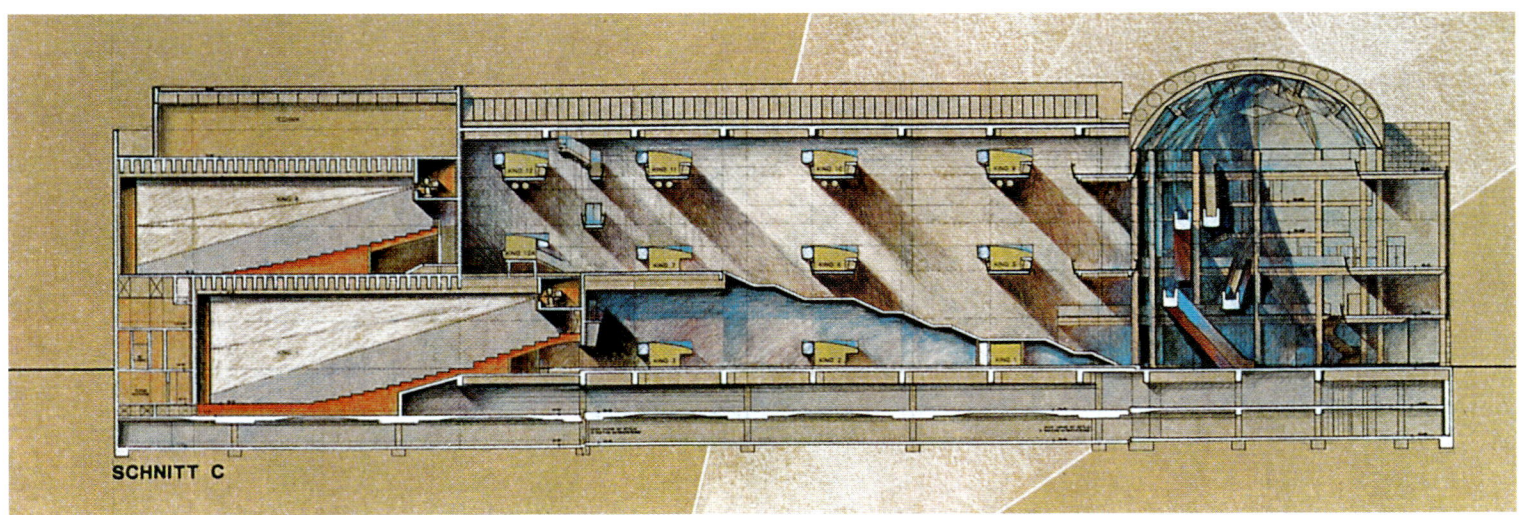

Detail of the canopy at the exterior of the Rotunda, a 100-foot high glass-enclosed entrance hall.

The view of the Rotunda. The various levels of the hall, interconnected by glass escalators, are ringed with galleries and enlivened by restaurants, bars, pool halls and shops.

Above, each theatre is entered over a bridge through a large mural. Right, the interior of one of the thirteen cinemas located on three levels. All seats are reserved by computer to reduce waiting time and the interior is painted black to heighten the film experience.

Opposite page, the dome at the top of the Rotunda reflecting the northern night sky through lights with a glass section that completes the starry sky at night.

26

Confederation Life Canadian Head Office
Toronto, Ontario

Towers have become symbols of the North American city - symbols of an urban way of life. They have given North American cities a vibrant vitality that has created an urban atmosphere distinctly different from that of European cities.

Confederation Life joins this proud heritage, yet conveys more than just the perfection of the modern office tower. Here, architecture not only pays homage to both form and technology, but also alludes to a uniquely Canadian architectural expression, firmly rooted in the history of Canada. The building evokes memories of the Canadian parliament buildings and the original Canadian Pacific Railway chateaux built shortly after Confederation, and in essence, is the very symbol of Confederation. The architectural expression of Confederation Life should continue to be a part of the future.

This transformation of past and present Canadian culture into architectural form, symbolically captures the historical foundation of the country and the solidity, strength, and permanence of Confederation Life - an architectural expression which so aptly matches the company's name.

Located on a unique site on an angled intersection, this 653,870-square foot complex relates both to the surrounding high-rise offices and apartments, as well as to the low-rise residential area.

The form of this complex appears as a series of conjoined turreted towers. Its verticality is emphasized through its massing, articulation, the interplay of glass and precast concrete, and particularly through the symbolic roof shapes which, silhouetted against the sky, create a significant and identifiable form in the Toronto skyline.

The transition from tall soaring towers to human streetscape scale is achieved through the use of low-rise horizontal elements, different size towers and turrets. The use of a sloped roof, punctuated rhythmically with residential dormers, reflects the residential scale of the neighbourhood to the East. The apex of the composition is crowned with a turret, reminiscent of the traditional mansions in nearby Rosedale to the North. The base of the office component on the west facade has a grand yet human scale; the 60-foot high base creates a grandeur appropriate for the entrance of a major Canadian corporate head office.

While incorporation of the most northerly residential property on Huntley Street would have allowed for a more typical office building configuration, the firm was opposed to this. Therefore, the first phase, the most substantial on the site, needed to achieve a certain prominence of image, as well as organization and had to allow for a future residential building along Huntley Street.

The Phase I Office Tower is 18-storeys high, has 12 typical office floors in excess of 30,000 square feet, three office floors of 7,000-square feet each, and is situated at the intersection of Jarvis and Mt. Pleasant, with the front entrance visible from Bloor Street. A bridge, with a turreted tower at either end, links the new building to the existing building and acts as a gateway to Rosedale, firmly rooting Confederation Life in the Bloor Street commercial district. This highly visible link is both a functional, aesthetic and symbolic link between the old and the new.

The Phase II Office Tower is 11-storeys high, with a typical floor plate of 10,000-square feet. It is located immediately north of, and is contiguous with, Phase I and extends the building towards Bloor Street. The Residential Component is a 32-unit four-storey element which faces the local residential neighbourhood.

The simplicity and elegance of glass and stone creates a timeless quality. The use of brick, a warm and inviting material, and the pristine quality of glass lends an air of translucence, efficiency and precision. The varied nature of the fenestration allows for a departure from the routine relentless repetition of window modules so typical of office towers.

Site plan and, bottom,
standard floor plans.

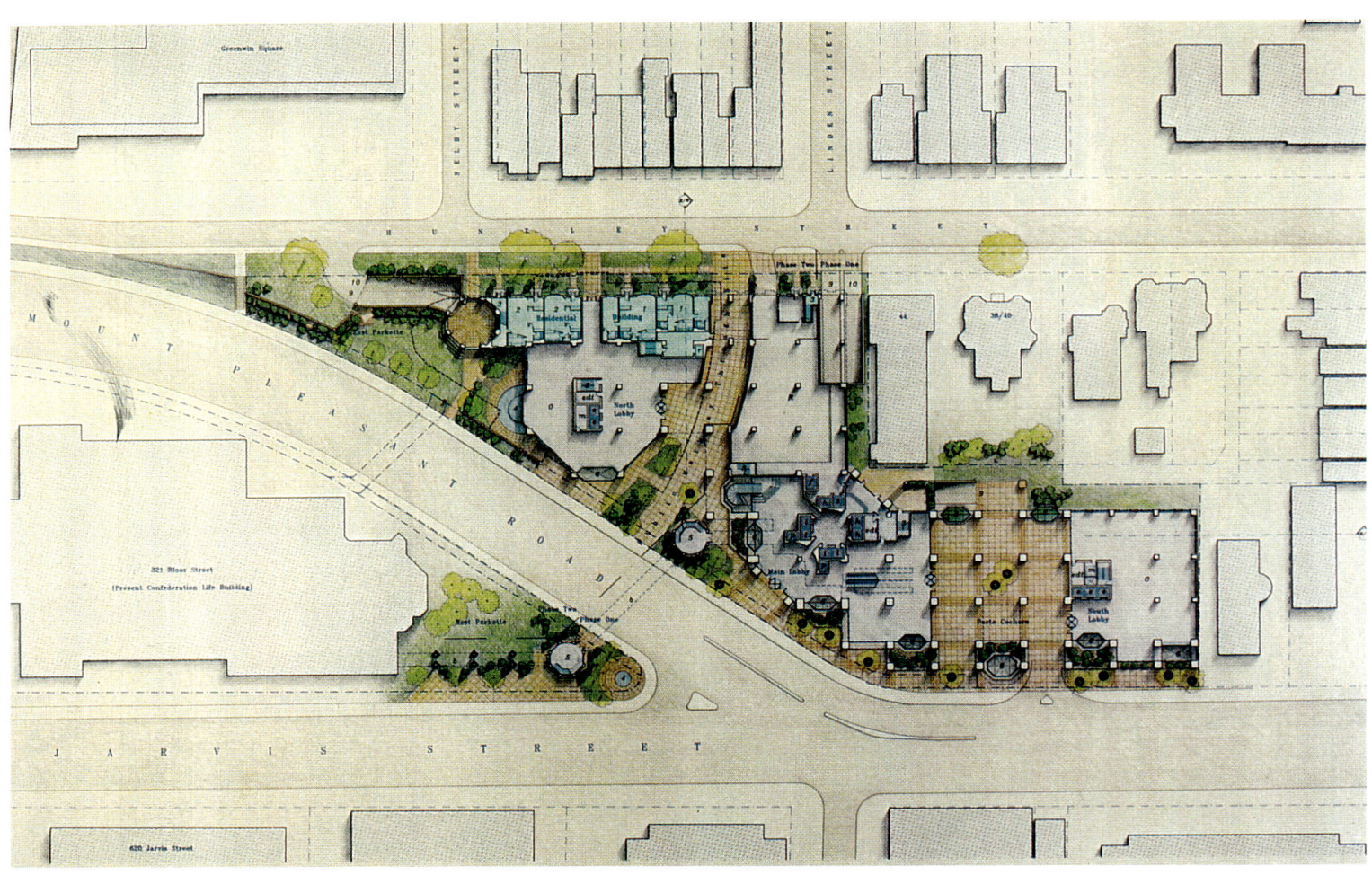

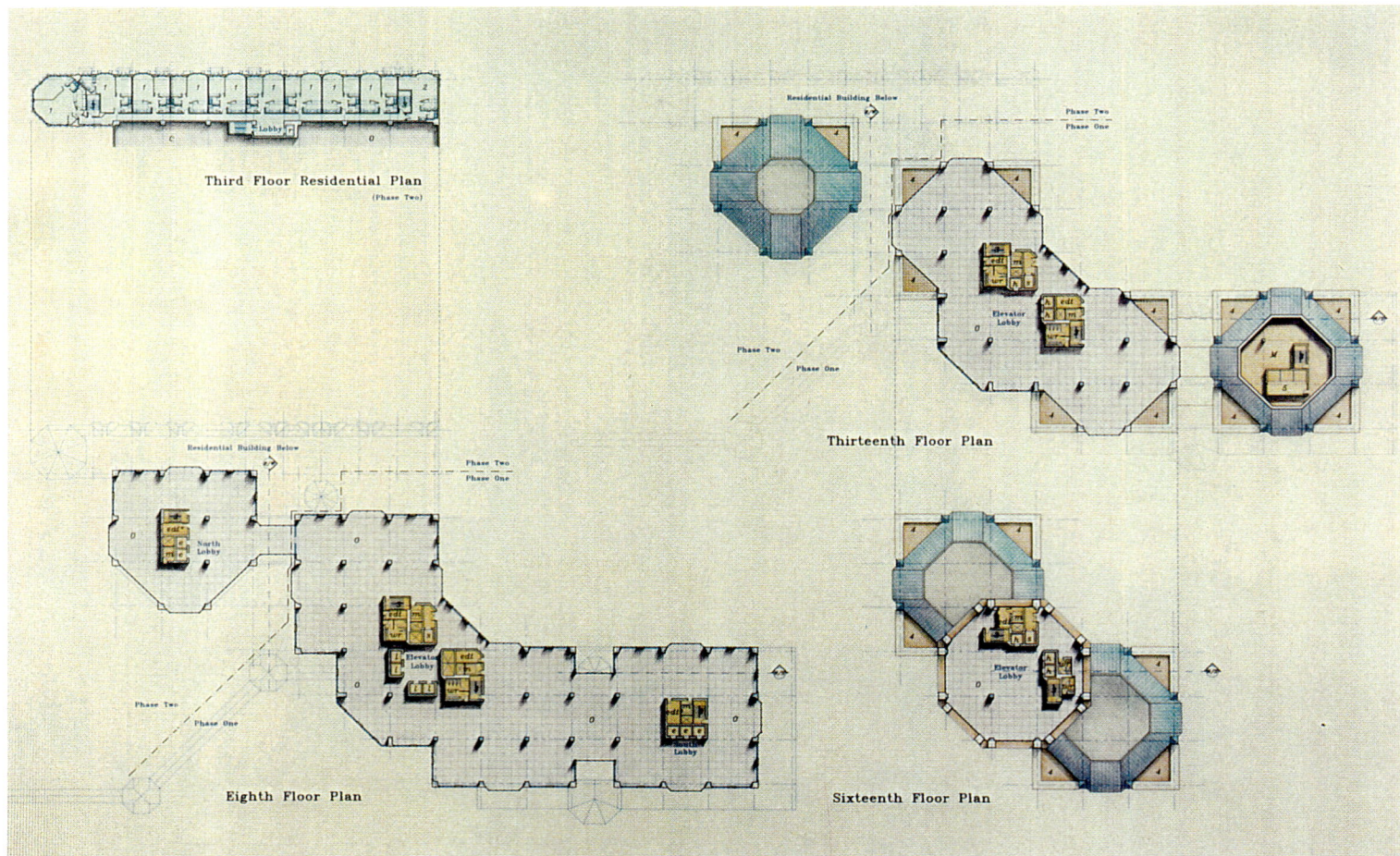

The entrance, featuring an arched iron girder, marks the transition from the vertical towers to the urban-scale roadways.

A view of project from the East.

The stairway in the building's central lobby.

Raymond F. Kravis Center for the Performing Arts

West Palm Beach, Florida

The Raymond F. Kravis Center for the Performing Arts sits like an acropolis on one of the highest and most visible points of West Palm Beach, overlooking Okeechobee Boulevard, which is lined with stately Royal Palms. As you drive along the boulevard, you get a spectacular view of the building and its image reflected in the waters of a pool in front of the Center. The lobby is expressed as a sculptural unity with carved cascading stairs, giving rhythm to the building form. The lobby sits above a classic baroque-like terrace with stairs descending into an ornamental pool. A wide glass canopy on the west side of the Center provides shelter for theatre guests in inclement weather and is clearly visible from Okeechobee Boulevard. The canopy also identifies the entrance to the parking garage, the Cohen Pavilion and the Rinker Playhouse. These three elements along with the main building create a memorable composition as you approach the complex.

From the beginning, it was agreed that the building should reflect the character of Florida's architecture which has in the past had many forms, often with classical overtones. One of the best-known and best-loved landmarks in Palm Beach is "The Breakers." With its two towers ascending above the building, it creates a strong visual memory for visitors and residents of Palm Beach alike. The two towers above the Center's stage house evoke this image.

The materials used are simple and stately, reflecting Florida's characteristic building materials. Rough hammered white stone is used at the base, a material found on many buildings in Florida. Italianate stucco, another material identified with Florida, has also been used. Green patinated copper roofs complete the composition. Special details add an interesting complexity to the building.

The theatre lobby is critical to the success of live performances. It must represent an auspicious beginning to the excitement of a performance, as well as give the audience an opportunity to see and be seen. In addition, the anticipated mature audience required elevators to reach their seats. Therefore, all audience and stage areas are fully accessible by elevators on all four levels, and each seat is either directly level with or only a few steps away from an elevator. Each level has its own washrooms and bar facilities, so that intermission time will not be spent searching for facilities or waiting in long lines.

In addition to the functionally flawless performance of the lobby, it creates a space which evokes the same emotional experience of the great theatres of the past. As well, the view through the windows of the lobby provide panoramic views of downtown Palm Beach and the ocean.

A number of conflicting demands had to be resolved to create an audience chamber that was not only outstanding for the performance of opera and ballet, but also for symphonic and electronically-reinforced performances. Since the Center would serve as a roadhouse, a large seating capacity had to be provided to make it attractive within the Florida circuit. After many meetings with the Board and user groups, the artistic quality of the space was determined to be the first priority, keeping in mind the provision of optimum seating. The goal was to create a space which would provide a sense of intimacy and in which each of the 2,189 seats would be as close to the stage as possible and provide excellent sight-lines and acoustics. It was also very important that the performers felt the audience participation and electricity.

During symphonic performances, the orchestra is seated on stage in front of a reflecting shield to take advantage of the stage volume for acoustic resonance. It was important, however, to maintain the feeling of an intimate space. The different acoustical environments required for various uses, are achieved by changing the relative quality of the walls in the audience chamber and by a special sound distribution chamber. The arrangement of the audience was conceived in such a way that even before the curtain goes up, the space represents a harmonious entity where the audience gives its own performance in anticipation of the coming event.

The Center has an engaging quality that will heighten any theatre experience. It evokes the warmth of a classical theatre, without reverting to repetitive eclecticism. The dome uniting the audience space, has on it an abstract mural created by Christina Zeidler, and gives the illusion of a night sky. The lighting recalls the sparkle of candlelights, fashioning classical details into a vision of our time.

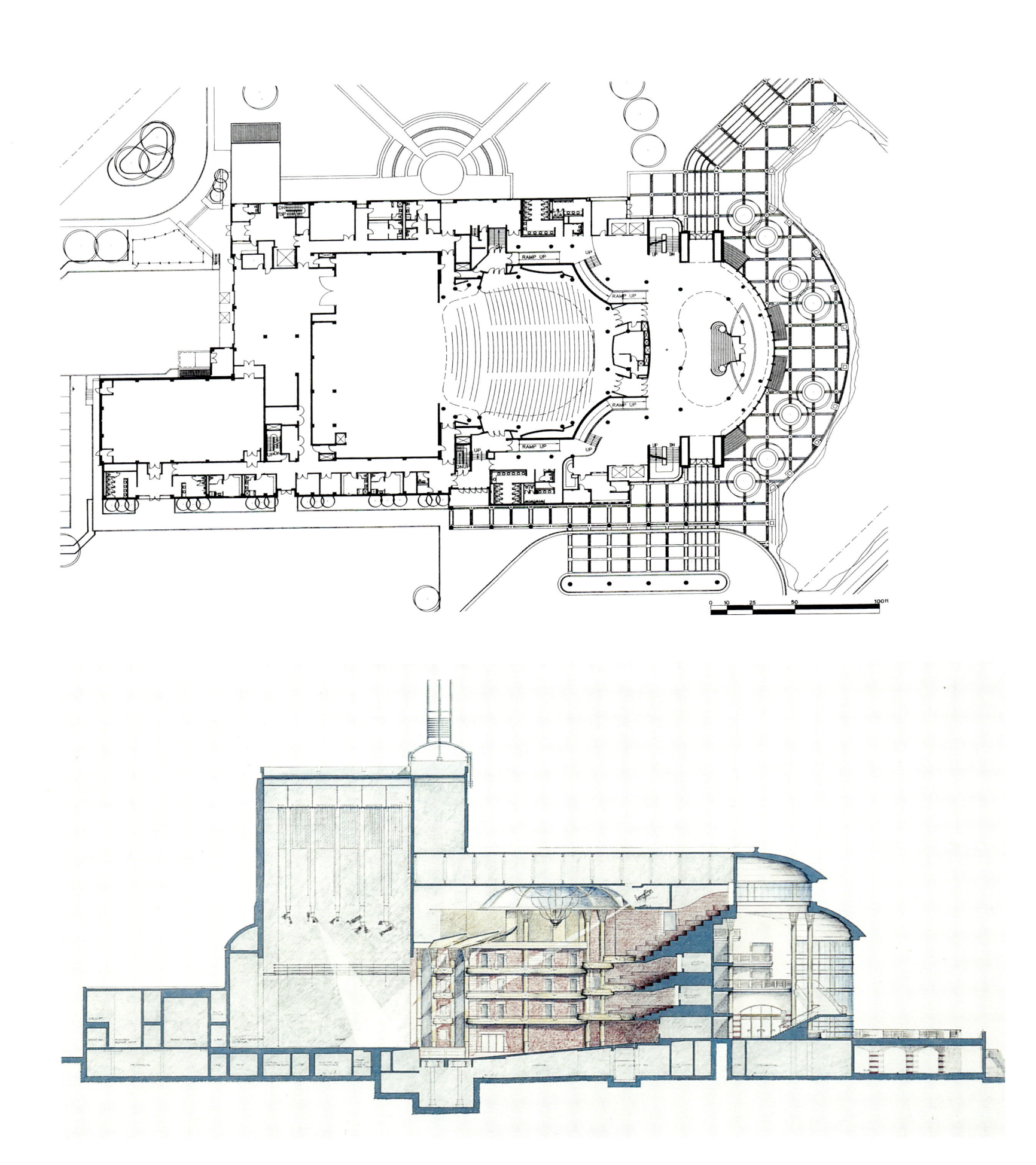

Plan of the orchestra level
and longitudinal section.

From bottom of page up, plans of the grand tier level, the mezzanine level, and loge level.

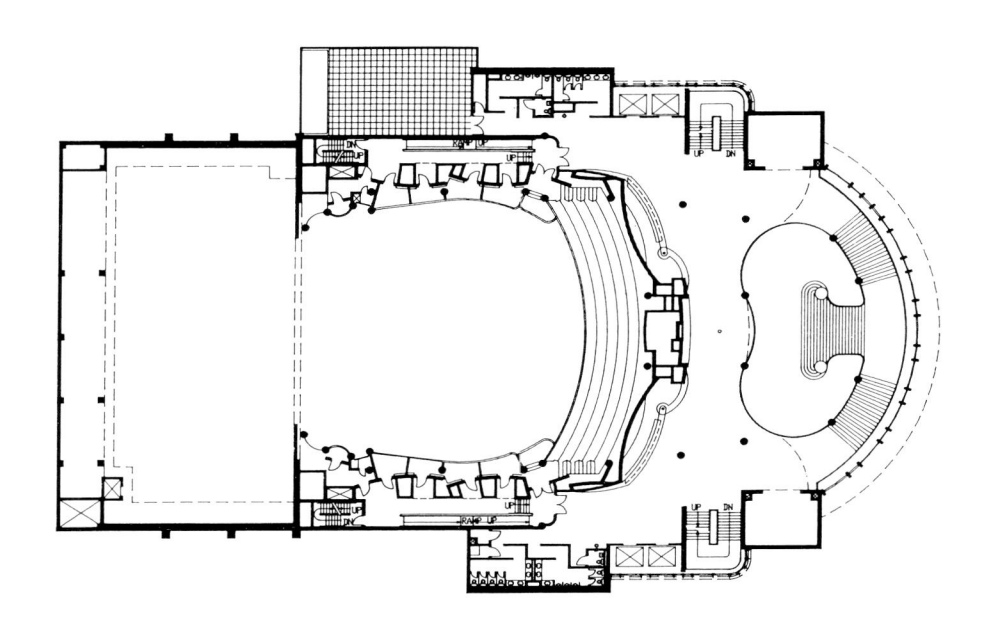

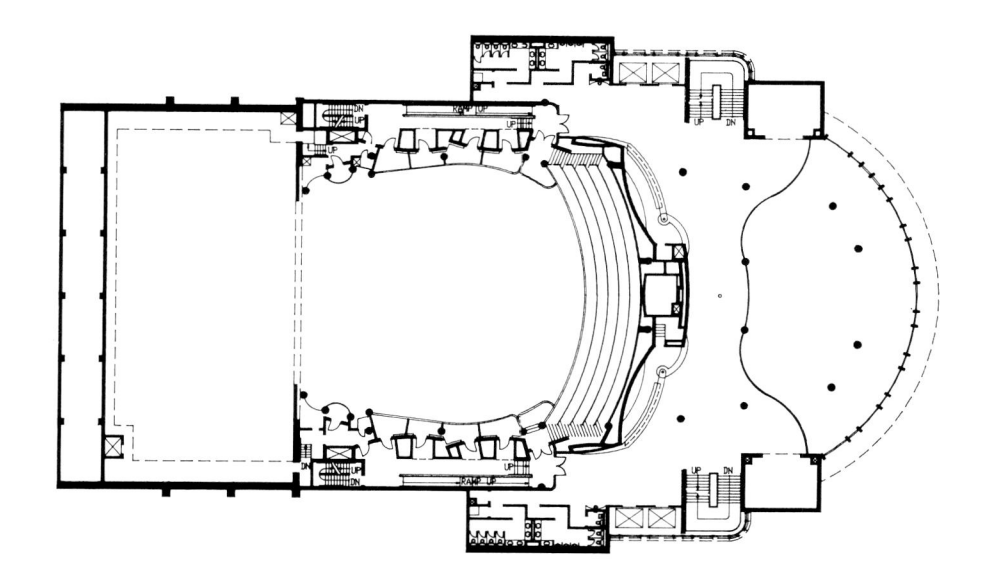

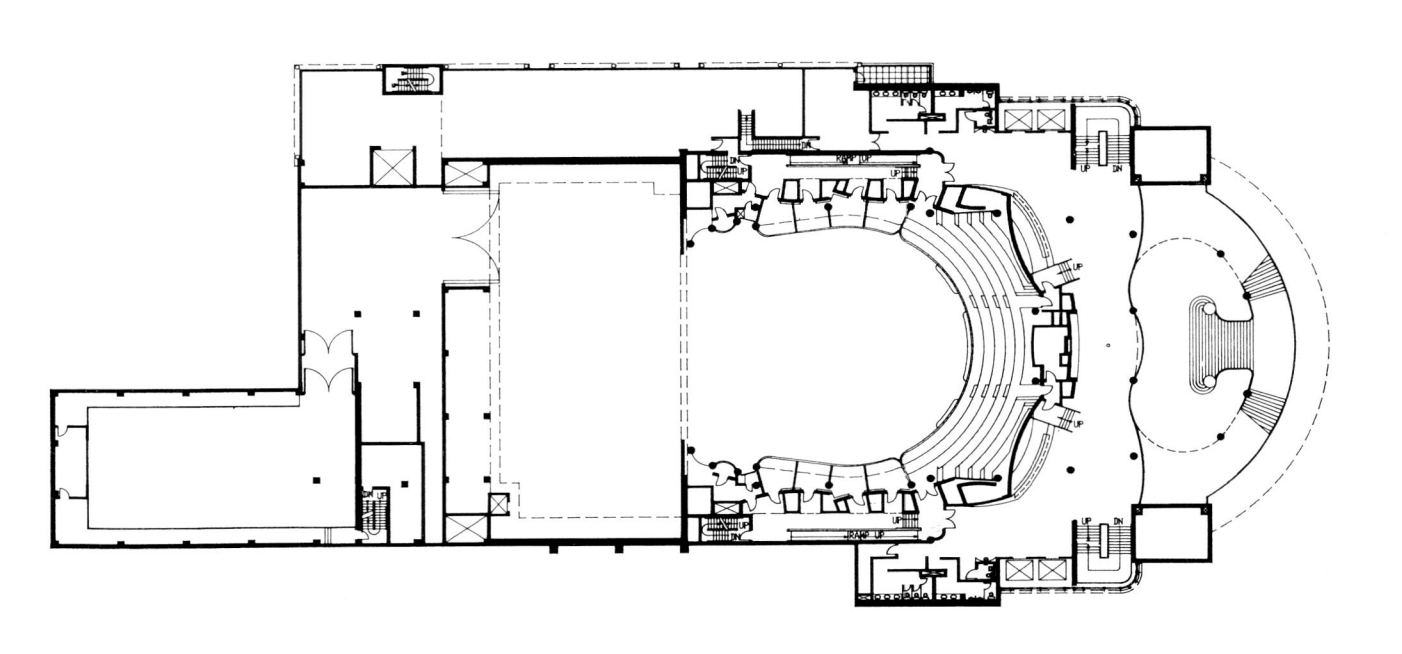

Nighttime view of the centre from Okechobee Boulevard showing the reflection of the water in the front pool.

Above, view of the main 2,189-seat hall from the stage. Right, the dome of the audience creates the illusion of a night sky through an abstract mural by Christina Zeidler, creating a dome out of a space that is for technical reasons wire mesh and concrete.

General view of the entrance hall. All upper levels look into and surround the ground floor lobby.

Detail of the stairs connecting the different levels of the entrance hall.

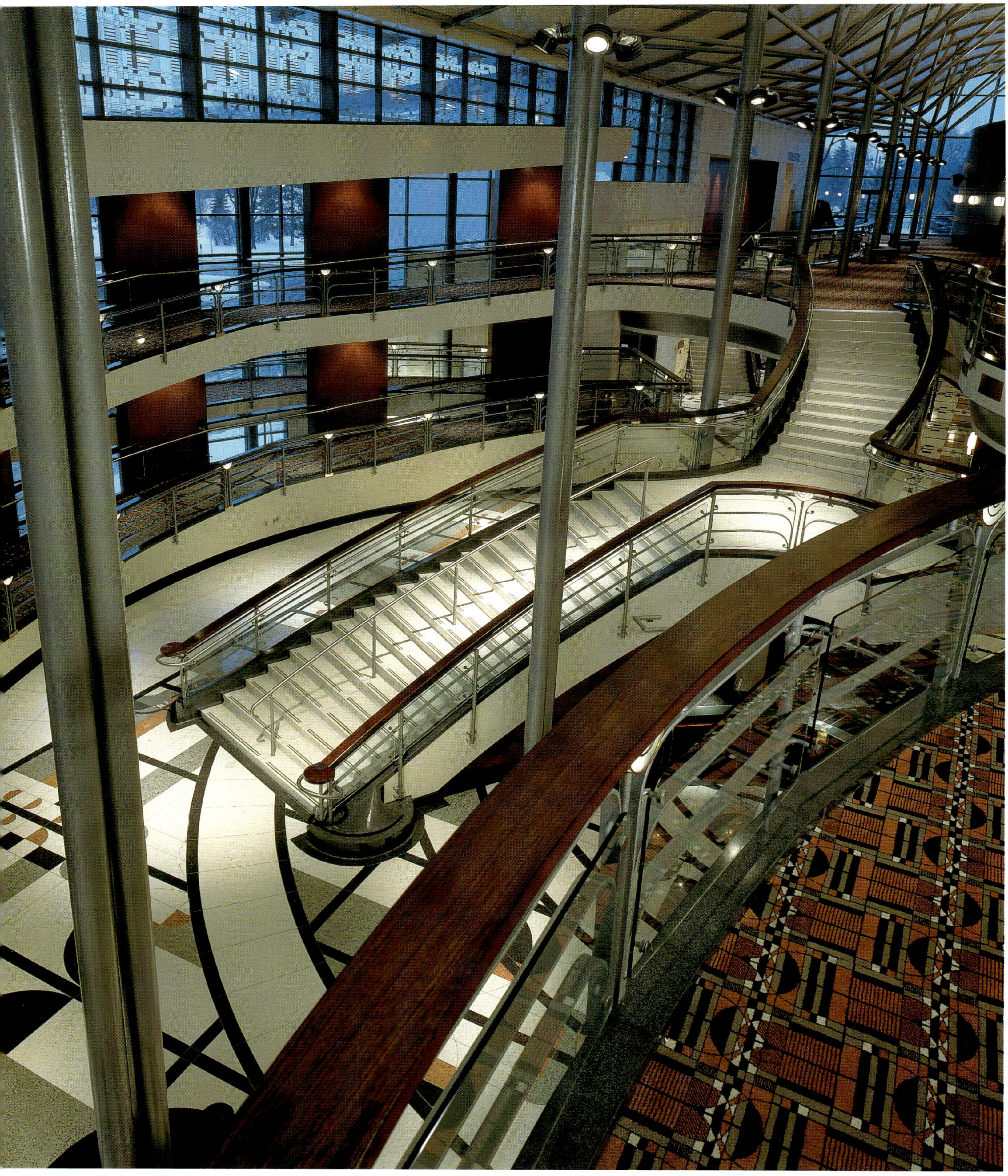

Ford Centre for the Performing Arts
North York, Ontario

Located in the heart of the city's downtown area, this 218,000-square foot complex, with its three theatres, combined lobbies and art gallery, is one of Canada's premier cultural facilities.

The architectural massing of the Centre was derived from the spatial-functional requirements of the theatres. Out of a two-storey podium rise the undulating forms of the main hall, stage tower and recital hall, symbolically manifesting the purpose of the building. The podium contains the lobby, experimental theatre, art gallery, and all of the required backstage facilities.

The theatres face north and are arranged side-by-side. The lobby is designed to allow either the full use of the total space for special events, or can be used as individual lobbies for each theatre. A semi-circular handicap ramp connects the first and second levels of the theatres. The linear quality of this lobby space is emphasized through an undulating roof which is supported by a series of tree-like columns and is slightly raised above the podium roof. This allows daylight to filter into the lobby during the day, while at night it emits the sparkle of interior lights, enhancing the appearance of the Centre. The lively activity of this space can be viewed from North York Boulevard through glass windows which enliven the street. A show window into the art gallery heralds its existence to those on North York Boulevard.

The largest and most ornate of the theatres, the Apotex Theatre, seats 1,856 people and was designed principally to accommodate roadhouse-type performances such as musicals, ballet, dance, and opera. The theatre provides a venue large enough to attract world-class performances while still maintaining its intimacy, excellent sight-lines and superb acoustics from each seat. It has a traditional horseshoe plan with two tiers of seating above the orchestra level. The audience is brought as close to the stage as possible with the levels wrapping around the sides in the form of box seats. The room is 92-feet wide and 92-feet long with a ceiling height of approximately 46-feet above orchestra level. Individuals in wheelchairs can be accommodated on the orchestra and dress circle levels. The finishing materials include marble base, brass trim, fabric and plaster walls and carpeted floors. The acoustic criteria was extremely stringent (PNC-15), the goal: all absence of background noise. Separate air handling units, mid-low air velocity with no terminals, and vibration isolation are some of the techniques used to achieve these standards. A unique feature of the Apotex Theatre is the air delivery system, used for the first time in North America. Air is supplied from below the theatre chairs, which are mounted on small perforated metal pedestals, and then drawn away through the ceiling dome to the mechanical room. The orchestra pit has a double lift which enables the stage to be set out into the audience or to seat the audience close to the stage when the pit is not required. Forestage rigging is provided with four motorized sets. The stage is 118-feet wide and 56-feet deep. The performance area is completely trapped (51-feet by 43-feet) and the floor has a masonite finish on a sprung wood assembly on neoprene pads. The grid iron is located 80-feet above the stage.

The George Weston Recital Hall is a tall shoe box-shaped room designed primarily for the presentation of unamplified musical performances. The audience is accommodated on two levels with the balcony wrapping around the performance area. Intimacy and sound energy are maintained by the close proximity of the audience to the stage, the room's shape and volume, and the massive construction of the walls, floors and ceilings. The hall's audience capacity is 1,025 people with accommodation for six wheelchairs at the orchestra level and four more at the balcony level. The hall is 69-feet wide, 115-feet long, and 59-feet high. Acoustic measures include a plaster reflector just above and in front of the performance area which directs sound forward to the audience, manually adjustable acoustic velour curtains on all walls to dampen sound, a removable concert wall around the performance area with variable reflective and absorptive surfaces, and a sprung wood floor. The performance area is approximately 30-feet wide and 52-feet long. A balcony surrounds this area and is able to accommodate a large chorus or a small symphony orchestra. To enhance performances, there are two bridges and a rigging trellis about the stage to accommodate performance lighting.

General views of the complex. The lively activities of the lobbies can be seen through glass windows and entrances along North York Boulevard and inject life into the street.

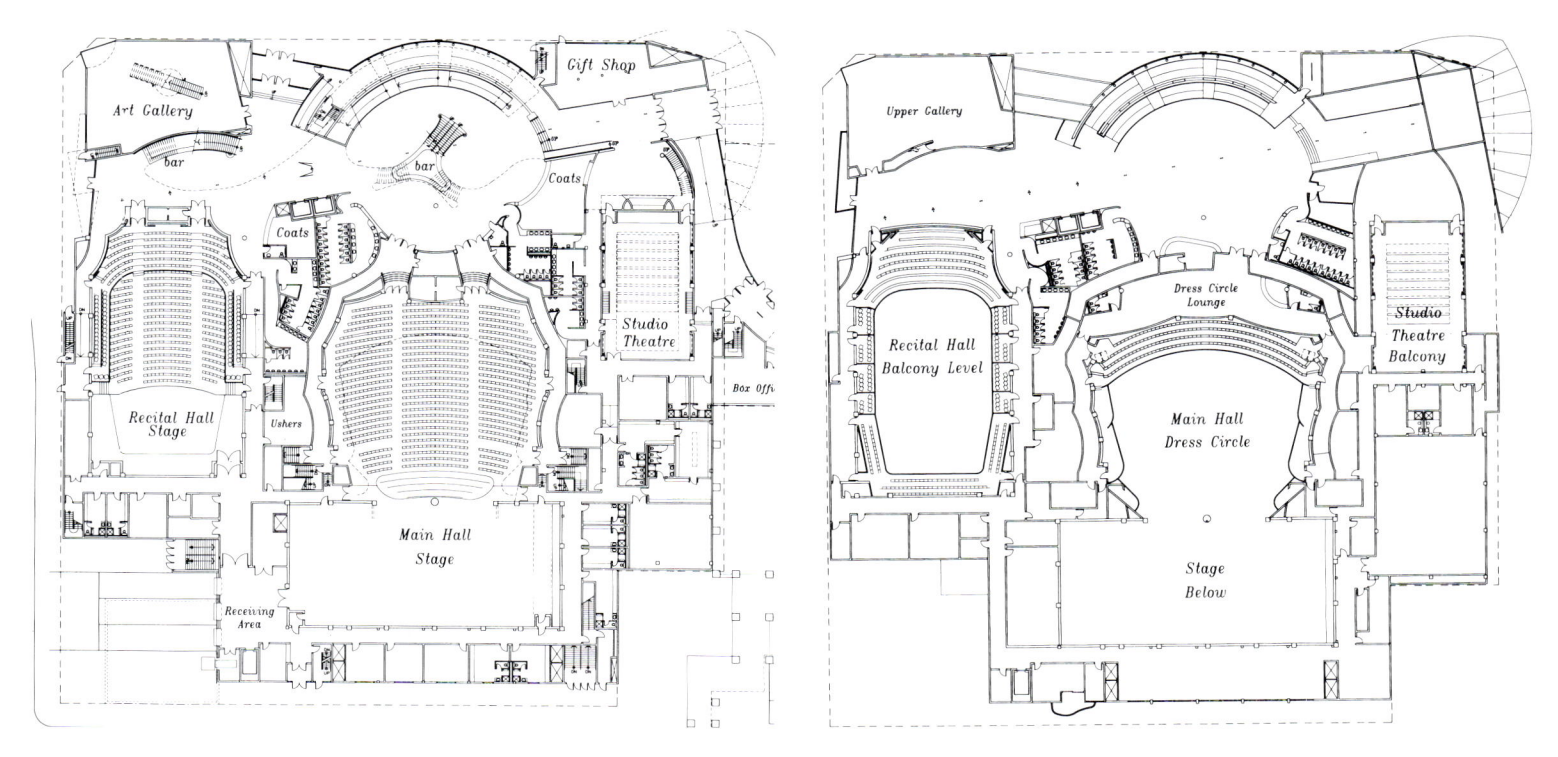

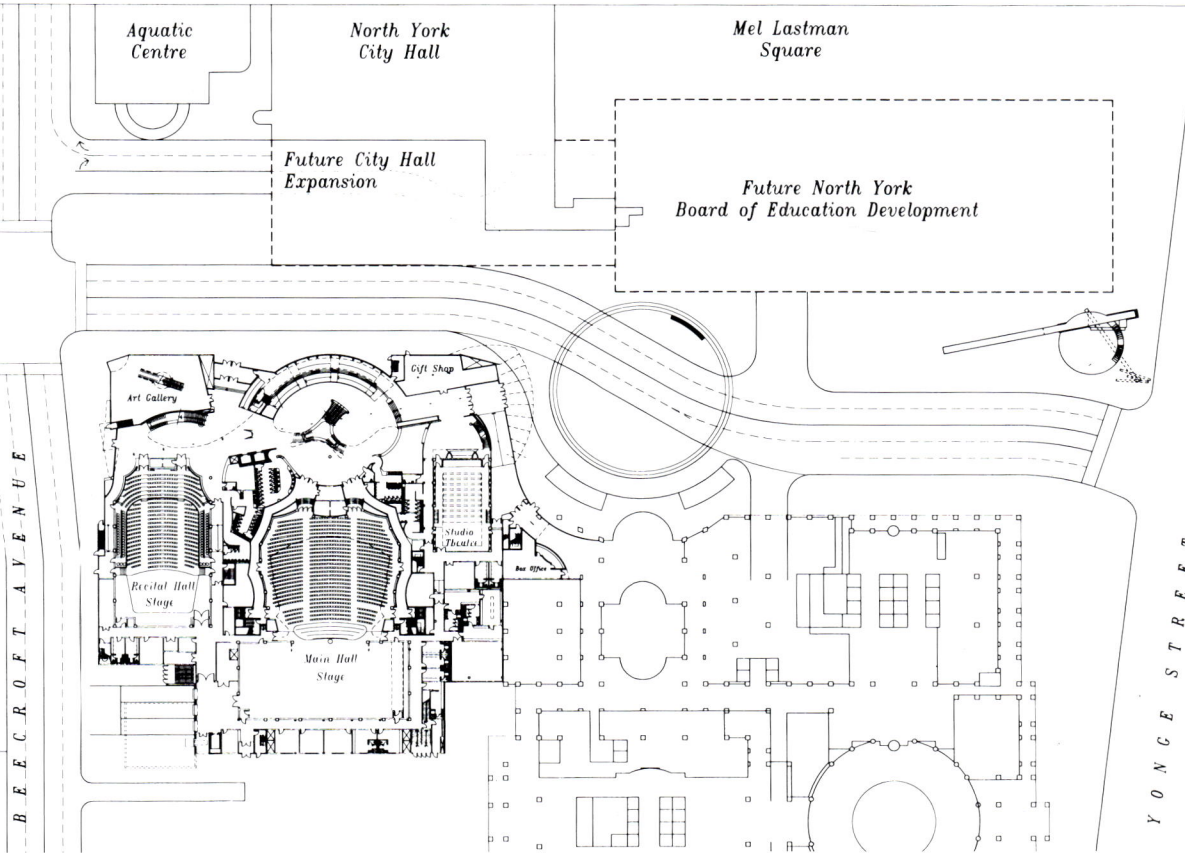

Above left, plan of the orchestra level, and, right, plan of the dress circle level. Centre, site plan. Bottom, lobby floor pattern which is a visual abstraction of musical overtones.

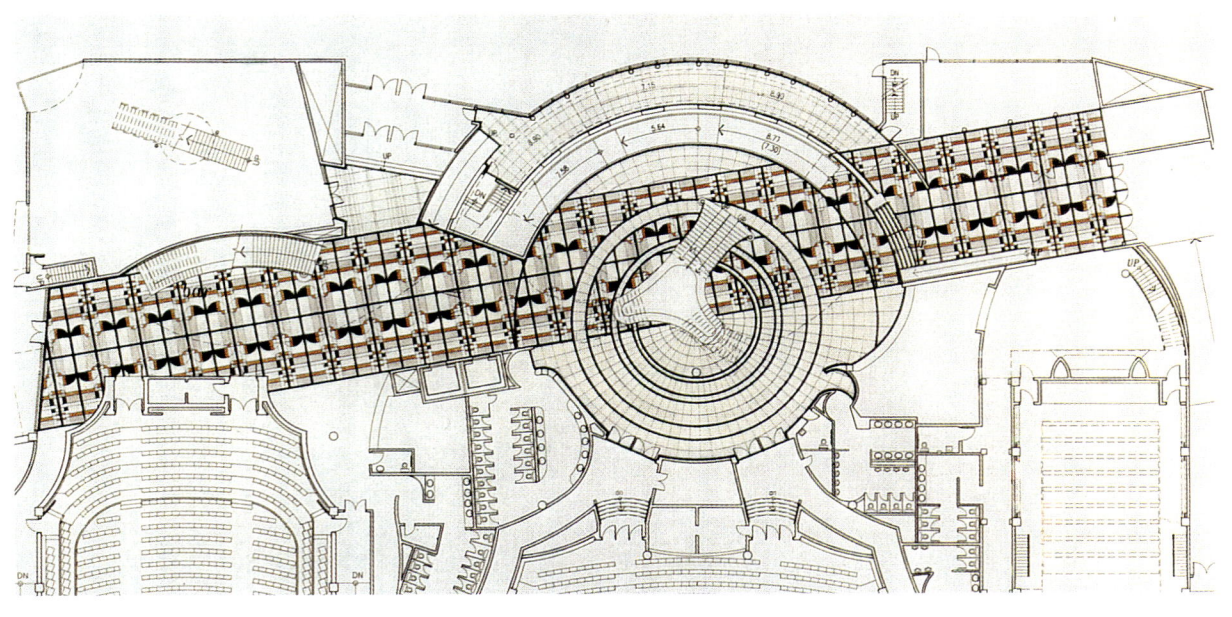

The main lobby of the complex, whose linear quality is emphasized through an undulating roof supported by a series of tree-like columns.

The Studio Theater has an audience capacity of 250 and is designed for experimental performances and community use/functions.

The George Weston Recital Hall, a tall shoebox-shaped room designed primarily for unamplified musical performances. This hall's audience capacity is 1,025.
Opposite page, the main hall, which seats 1,856 and is designed to accommodate musical, ballet, dance and opera. The centre chancelier conceals the lights bridge for the stage.

48

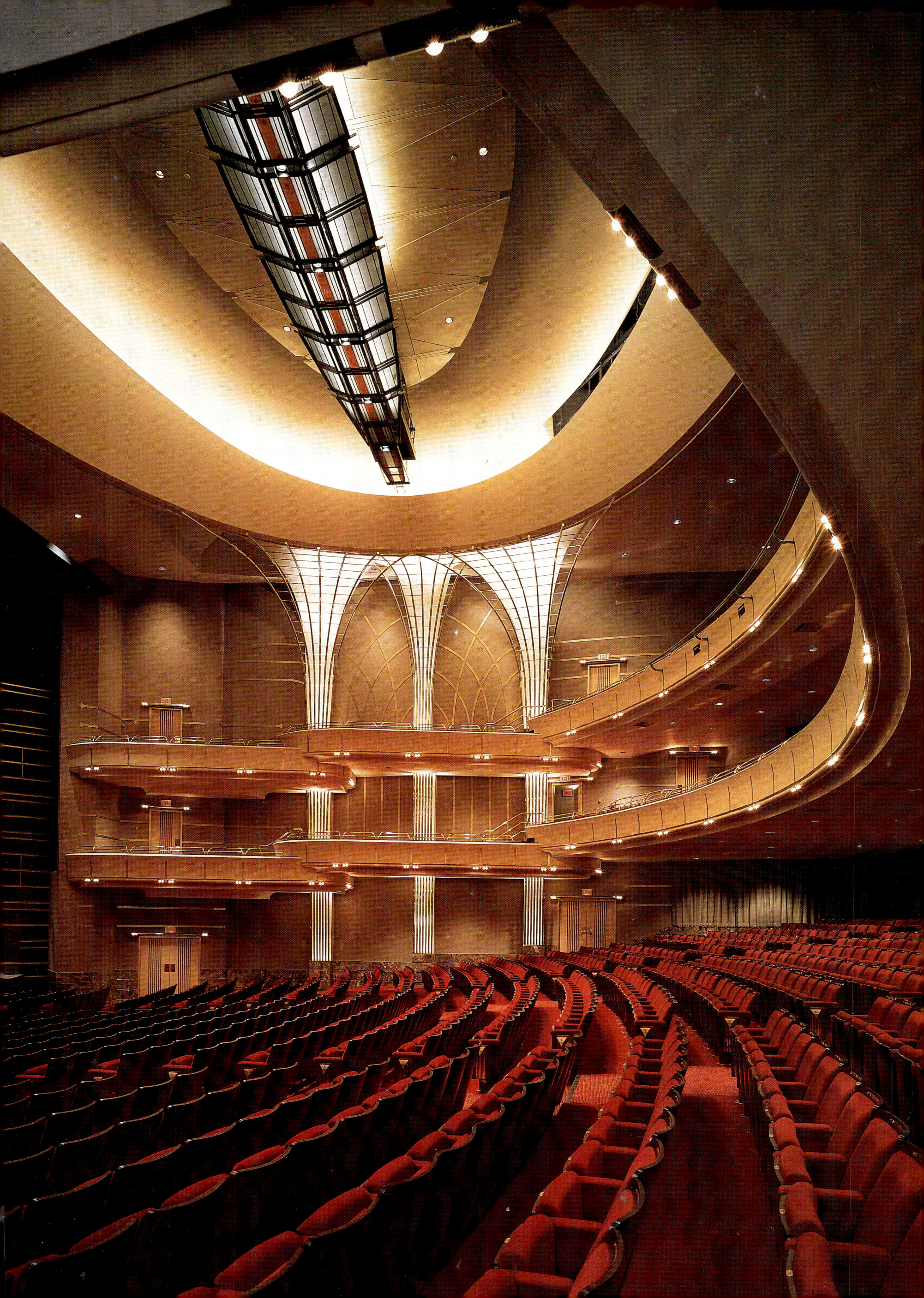

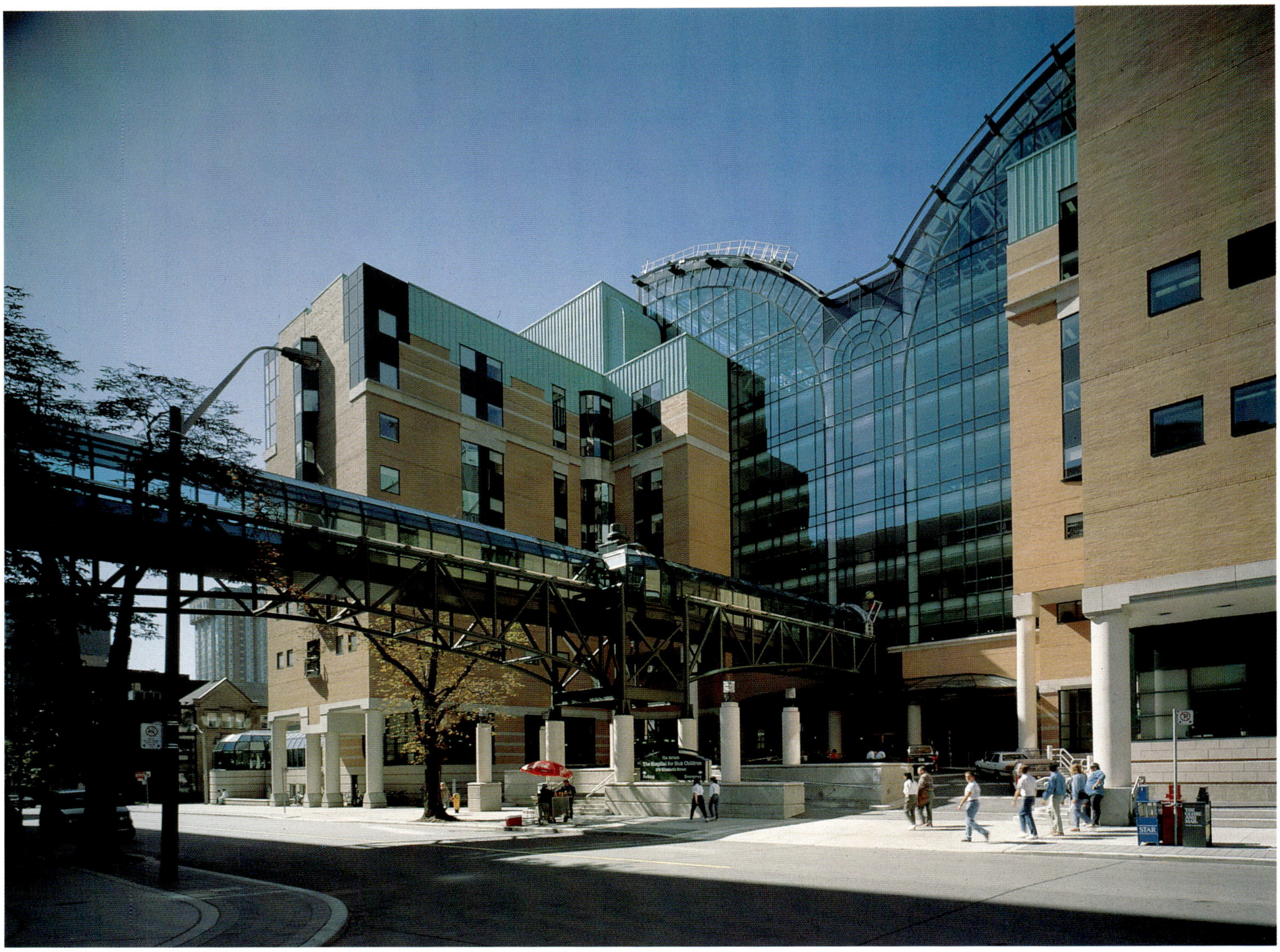

The Hospital for Sick Children
The Atrium, Toronto, Ontario

In the past, a series of additions to this famous children's hospital resulted in various building structures that covered a tight downtown site, many were in urgent need of upgrading. The problems which needed to be addressed were: how to find additional space on the existing site, how to connect the new and the old buildings into a well-functioning hospital, and, most importantly, how to achieve an environment that responded to the emotional needs of the sick children.

By demolishing an existing parking garage and decanting two old buildings, half of the site was freed for the new programme. The new building included: Admitting, Emergency, Ambulatory Case, Radiology and Magnetic Resonance Imaging Areas, a Surgical Suite with fourteen operating rooms, Surgery Support Areas, Pediatric and Neonatal Intensive Care Units, Service Laboratories (such as Biochemistry, Hematology and Pharmacy), Material Management, Receiving, Central Stores and Linen Areas, a Central Sterile Room, a Cafeteria with seating for 722, a Kitchen, a Main Entrance, and a total of 572 beds in the New Patient Wing, and replaced all of the inpatient units in the existing facility. Each typical floor has 96 inpatient beds and four nursing stations.

The new addition covers an area of 1.201 million square feet. The eight-level building occupies 790,650-square feet of space, and a four-level below-grade parking garage with 950 parking spaces, occupying 410,170 square feet.

On the exterior, the new addition blends with the existing urban situation in its massing and materials. The exterior envelope is brick with renaissance stone reveals at the base. Through such interesting details, the new facades relieve the monotony of the existing buildings without affecting the coherence of the complex.

The design of the atrium was the result of a rigorous investigation into the most effective building forms. The accepted programme anticipated relocating the most urgent services of the hospital into the new structure and freeing up most of the existing buildings for services which might be required in the future.

By their very nature, teaching hospitals are rather large institutions which never present a clear picture of their interior organization. They seem to lose both their staff and visitors in a maze of corridors. The atrium design visually explains the organization of the hospital - from there one understands where to go and how to get there. This creates a sense of comfort for both users and staff. Nothing is more reassuring than a clear sense of orientation in a large complex.

In addition to the above, the atrium provides other beneficial effects that are important in a hospital environment: it serves to integrate the surrounding space, provides emotional benefits to patients, provides a green space of hope during all four seasons (including Toronto's harsh winters) and, contrary to what one might think, the atrium space is actually more economical in terms of capital and operating costs than traditional solutions, due to the reduction of exterior surfaces.

Increased pedestrian traffic from the east end of the city meant that a new entrance was required on that side of the hospital. An interior "main street" links this new entrance with the hospital's public space and activities (cafeteria, gift shops, etc.) and with the existing west entrance at University Avenue, as well as to the clinics and research departments in the existing buildings.

A unique feature of the hospital is the creation of single-patient rooms for each child. Each room is equipped with a private bathroom and sofa-bed so that a parent may spend the night with the child. This arrangement has proven to be most desirable for the patient and very effective for the hospital. The new rooms have eliminated the frequent need to move the patient during the various stages of the healing process, as was required in the past.

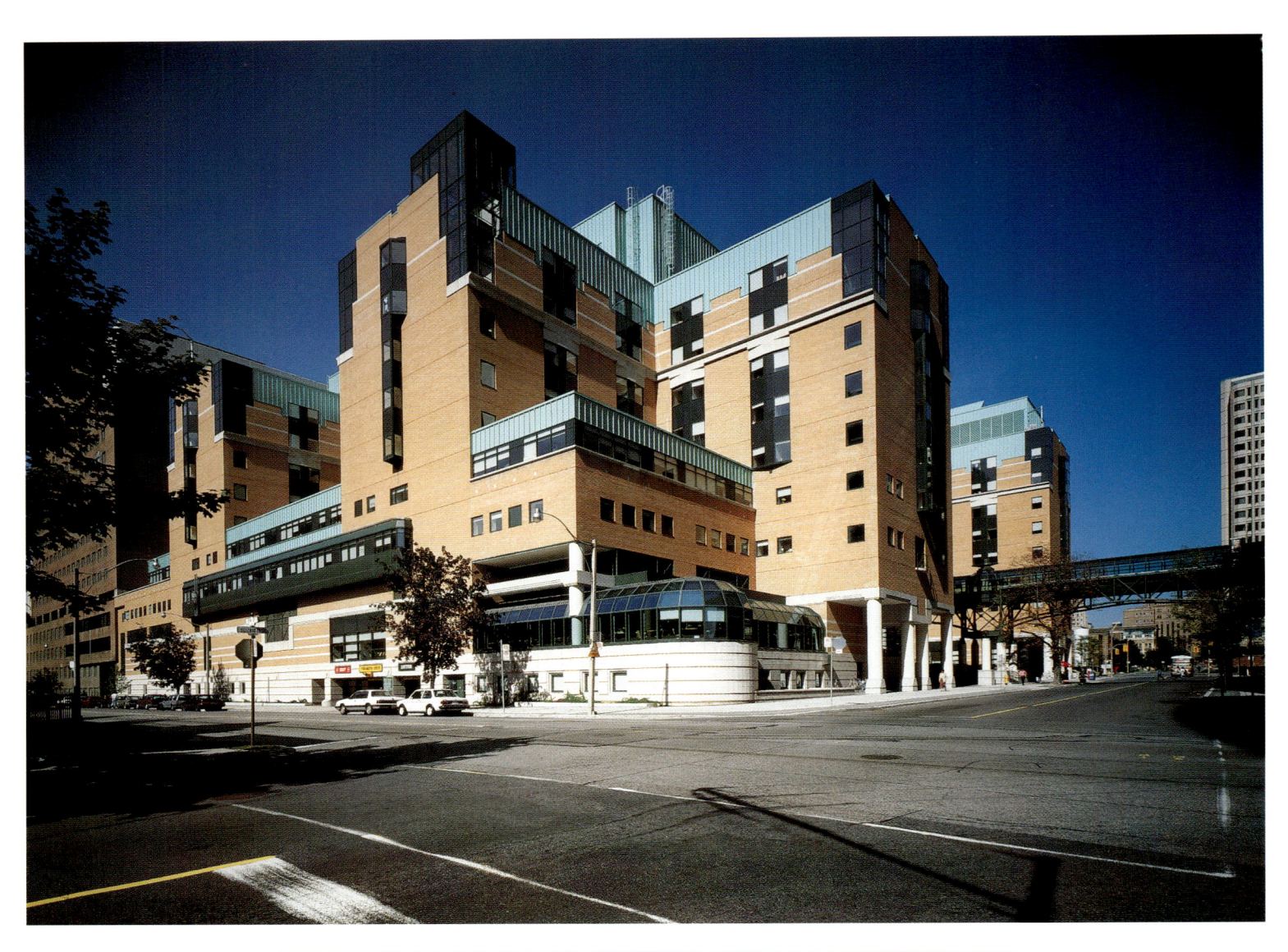

Outside views of the new building, which is mainly clad with bricks and Renaissance stone.
The main building has eight floors above ground level housing the hospital facilities and four underground levels for parking.

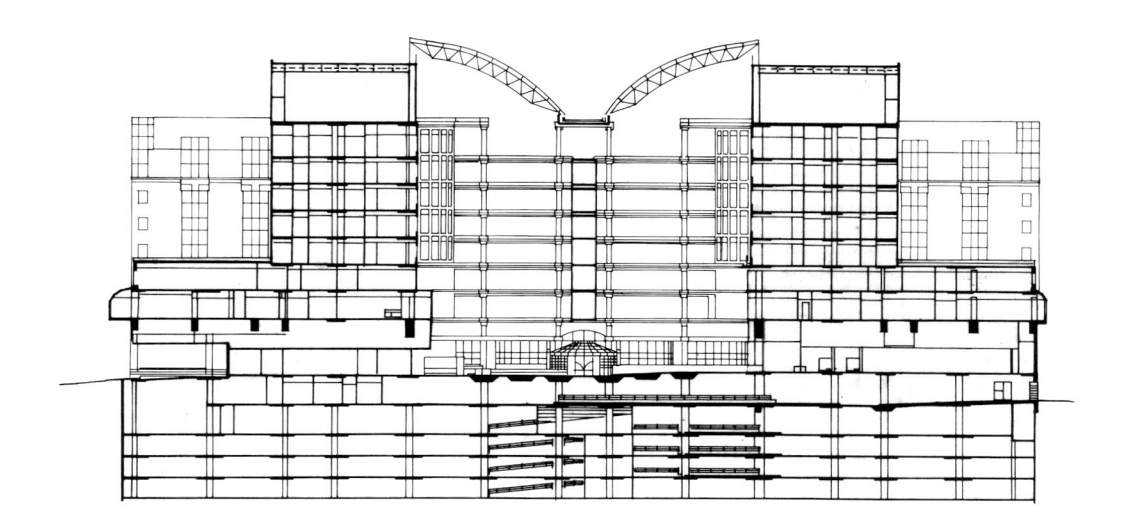

Bottom of page, left, ground-floor plan and, right, plan of a standard floor from the fourth to eighth levels. Centre, site plan. Left, cross section looking east. Note the separation of the vertical traffic through glass elevators in the middle of the atrium for visitors and inside patient and service elevators between the nursing units.

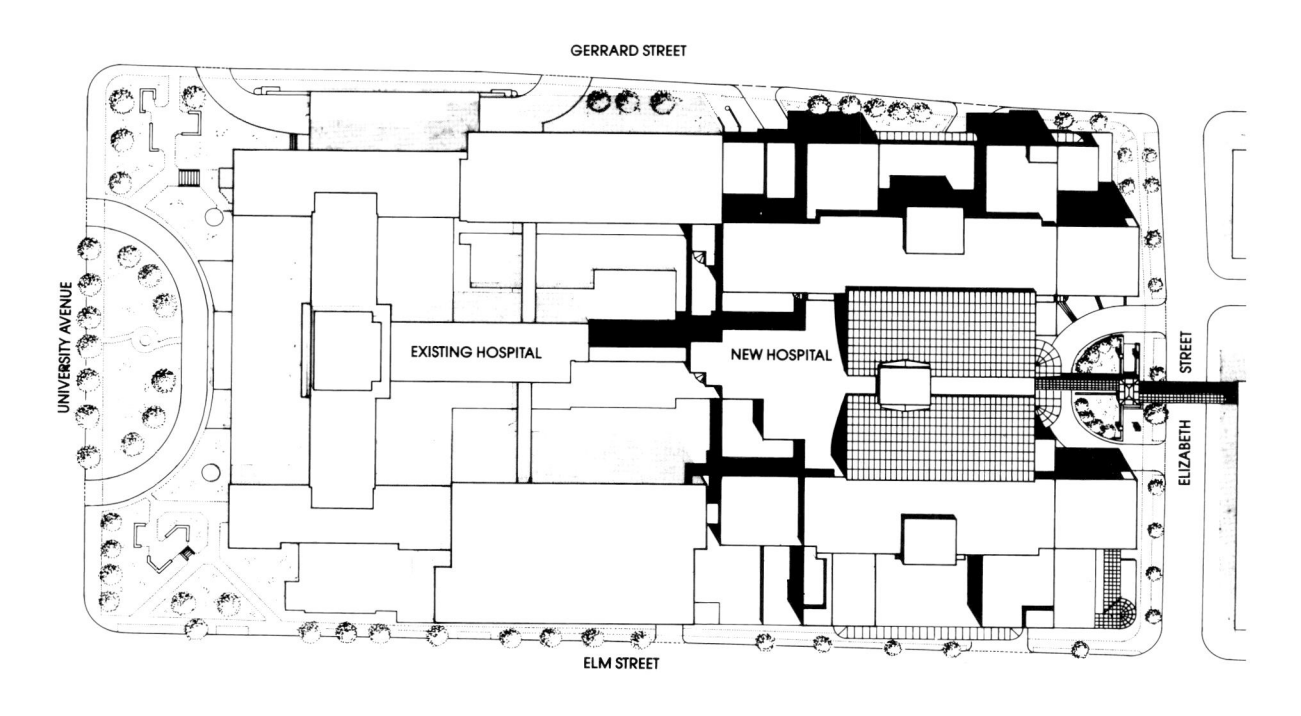

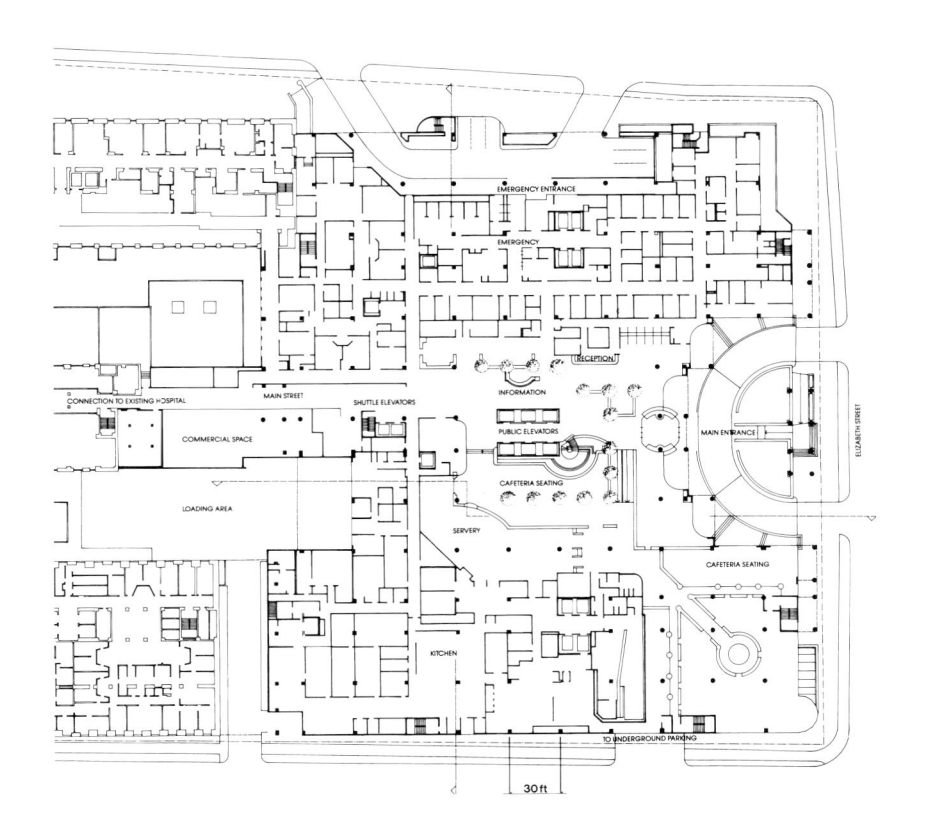

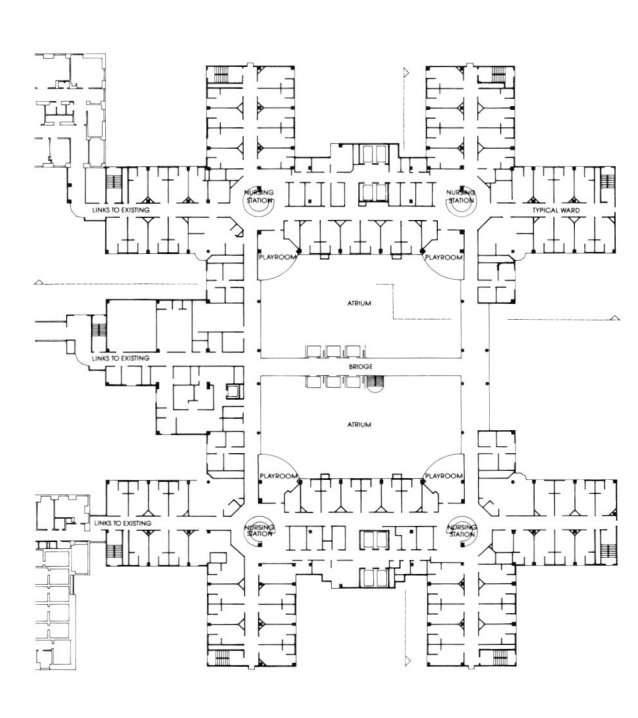

The glass bridge joining together the new and old buildings. Below, the central atrium at a centre focus with a view into the cafeteria section.

54

The large atrium is designed to visually organise the hospital complex. Here is the view into the Admitting and Entrance areas; at the left side are the public glass elevators, at the right rear the windows of the play areas in the five nursing floors.

Above, perspective view from inside the glass corridor traversing the atrium. Right, one of the single children's rooms equipped with a bed-settee for one of the parents.
Opposite page, view into the atria with a moving sculpture. The large windows of the corner are the children's play rooms.

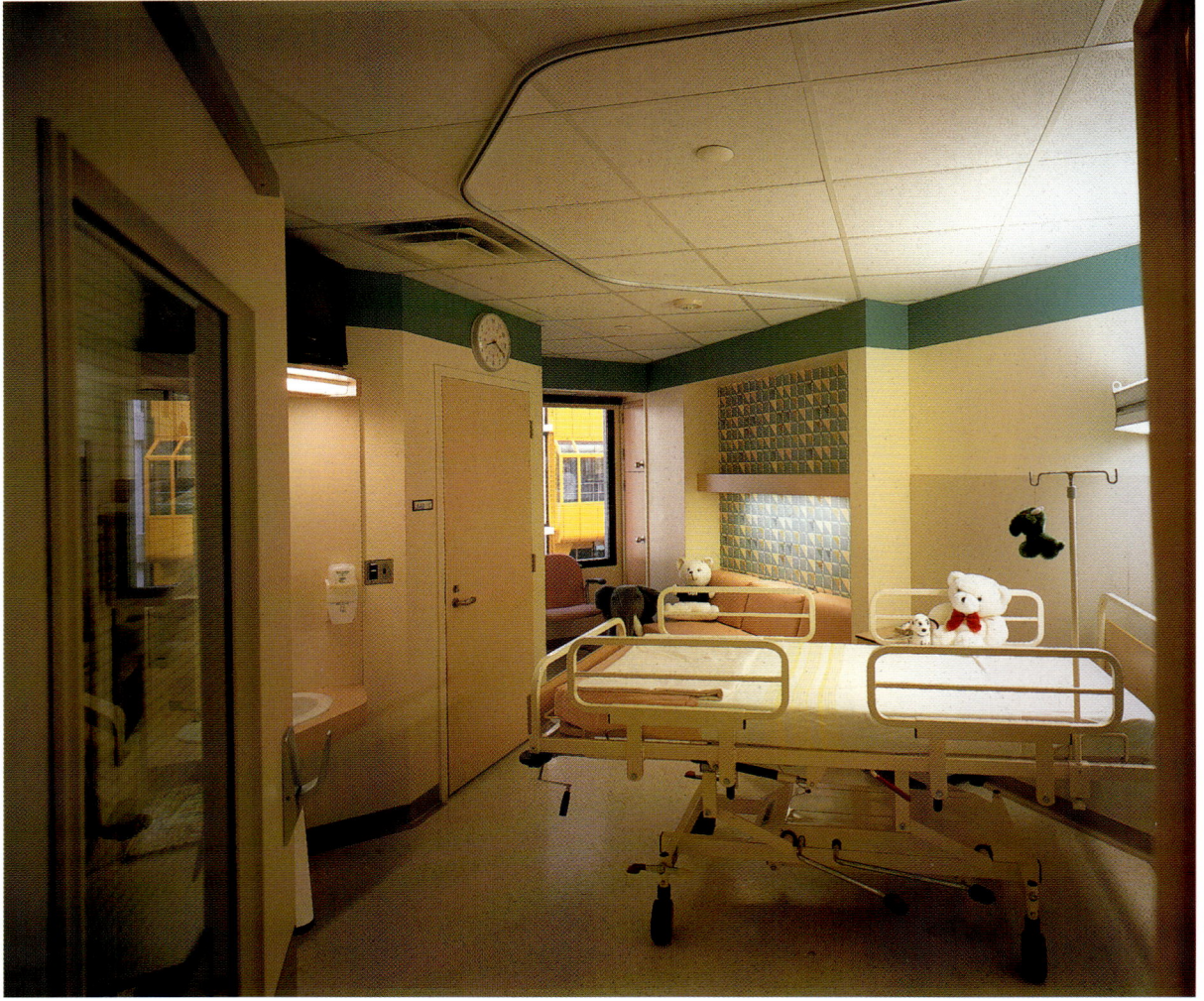

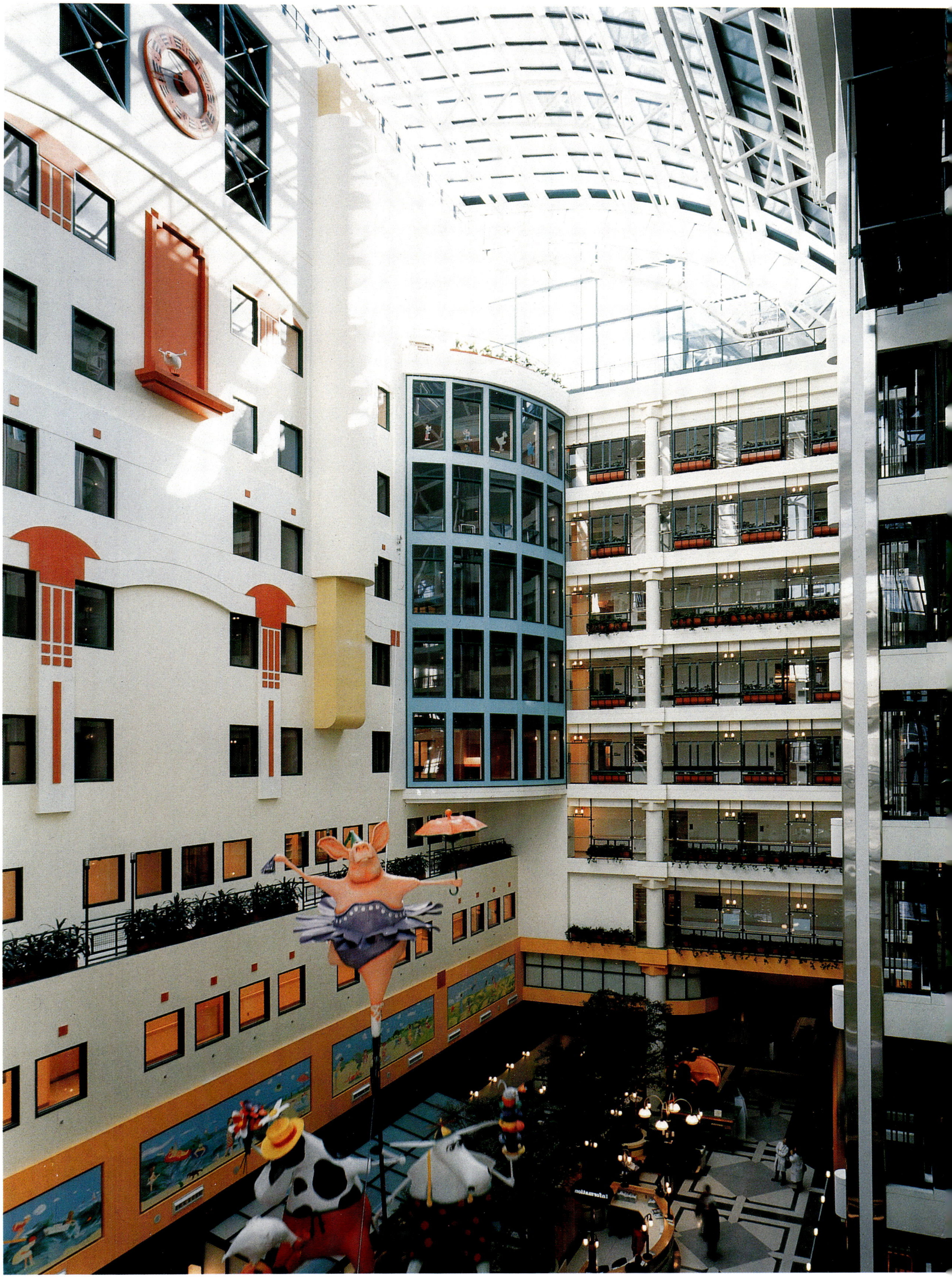

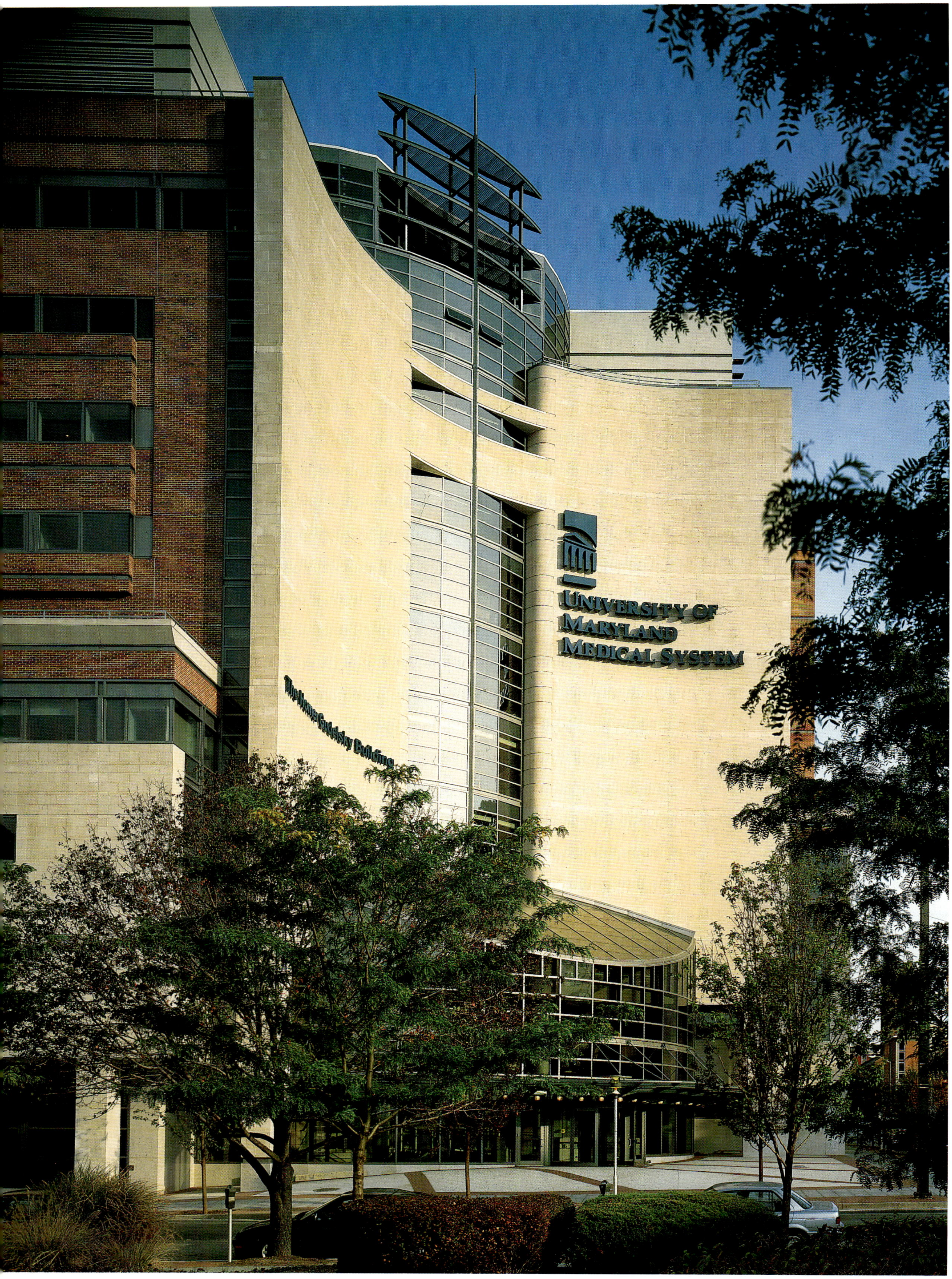
UNIVERSITY OF
MARYLAND
MEDICAL SYSTEM

University of Maryland Medical System The Homer Gudelsky Building
Baltimore, Maryland

In 1984, the University of Maryland Hospital previously a public hospital, became a private non-profit institution, and the beginning of a long-range plan to upgrade and expand its physical plant was conceived. The master plan, commissioned in 1986, identified a three-phase, $210-million programme to upgrade the hospital's facilities and achieve its targeted standards of excellence for service.

The first phase consisted essentially of renovations to the existing building. Phase II included: a clinical tower for Radiation Oncology; inpatient beds for Cancer Care, Neurocare and Cardiac Care and an Ambulatory Surgery Centre.

The Homer Gudelsky Inpatient Building is the clinical component of this programme. At the outset of the project, the University of Maryland Medical System (UMMS) established very clear priorities as to what it wanted to achieve: a "signature" building which enhanced the institution's public image and conveyed a message of technical competence and that of a healing environment; a building which fit in harmoniously within its architectural context and respected the UMAB Campus design guidelines; the revitalization of the West Baltimore neighbourhood; and a functional building which provided not only for the users', visitors' and staff's physical needs, but also catered to their emotional needs.

The Gudelsky Building occupies a prominent corner of the city's street grid in Baltimore's west end and is highly visible to the public: the site is located across the street from Davidge Hall (significant historically as the original School of Medicine), and is also visible from the new baseball stadium.

The massing of the new building relates to the scale of Davidge Hall and to the future medical library, which is to be located on the south side of Lombard Street, and also to the existing buildings.

With the addition of the new inpatient tower, the circulation of both the new and the old parts of the hospital were completely reorganized. The Gudelsky Building was linked to the north hospital entrance by creating a gallery. Eventually, this street-gallery will extend westward into Phase III along Lombard Street. This new gallery allows access to all of the vertical circulation cores of the existing hospital without interfering with the existing services, circulation of staff and patients, and material delivery. It also affords easy orientation for visitors and outpatients. The atrium created between the Gudelsky Building and the existing hospital has become part of this street-gallery and also serves as an orientation device.

The Gudelsky Building achieves efficiency by separating circulation of the public and of services. The public elevators open onto the atrium and are immediately visible to the visiting public who circulate at the outer edge of the atrium, along public areas such as the reception desks and the visitor lounges. The internal circulation area is reserved for staff, patients and material handling only, and is accessible via a separate bank of elevators. This layout achieves not only functional efficiency, but also creates an environment that assists emotionally in the healing process. The cool green gardens in the atrium and the entrance rotunda also soothe the stress and anxiety associated with illness benefiting both visitors and staff.

The outside skin of the building, composed of brick and synthetic stone masonry with metal channel reveals, was designed to harmonize with the surrounding buildings and respects the UMAB campus design guidelines, while using a contemporary formal vocabulary. The envelope is also designed to meet the stringent technical requirements of a medical facility in terms of air and vapor permeability. The atrium is covered with a segmented, sealed-unit glazing system which is integrated at the north and west ends with a curtain wall system. The building meets all ADA requirements.

The main energy conservation feature of the building, besides passive measures such as insulation in walls and roots, is the atrium itself. Enclosing the space between the two buildings not only saved on capital costs but also reduces operational costs, as walls which would have been outside walls, are now interior walls.

From bottom of page up, site plan, showing reorganisation of interior traffic into separate public circulation and staff and patient circulation, plan of the first level, top left, plan of the fourth level, and, right, cross section. Opposite page, the large central gallery surrounded by the existing building to the right and the new tower to the left at back, creating a clear visual arrangement of orientation.

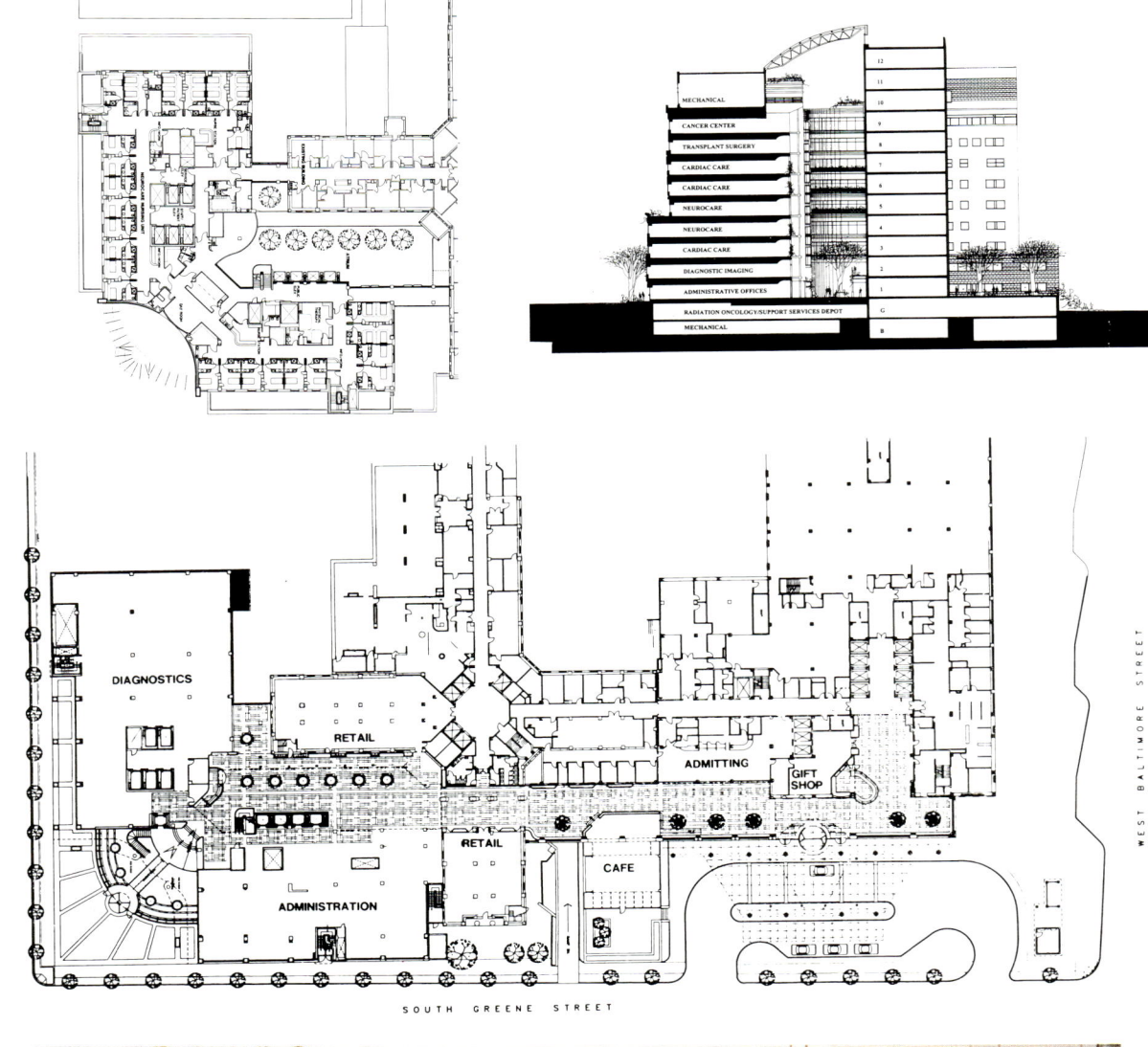

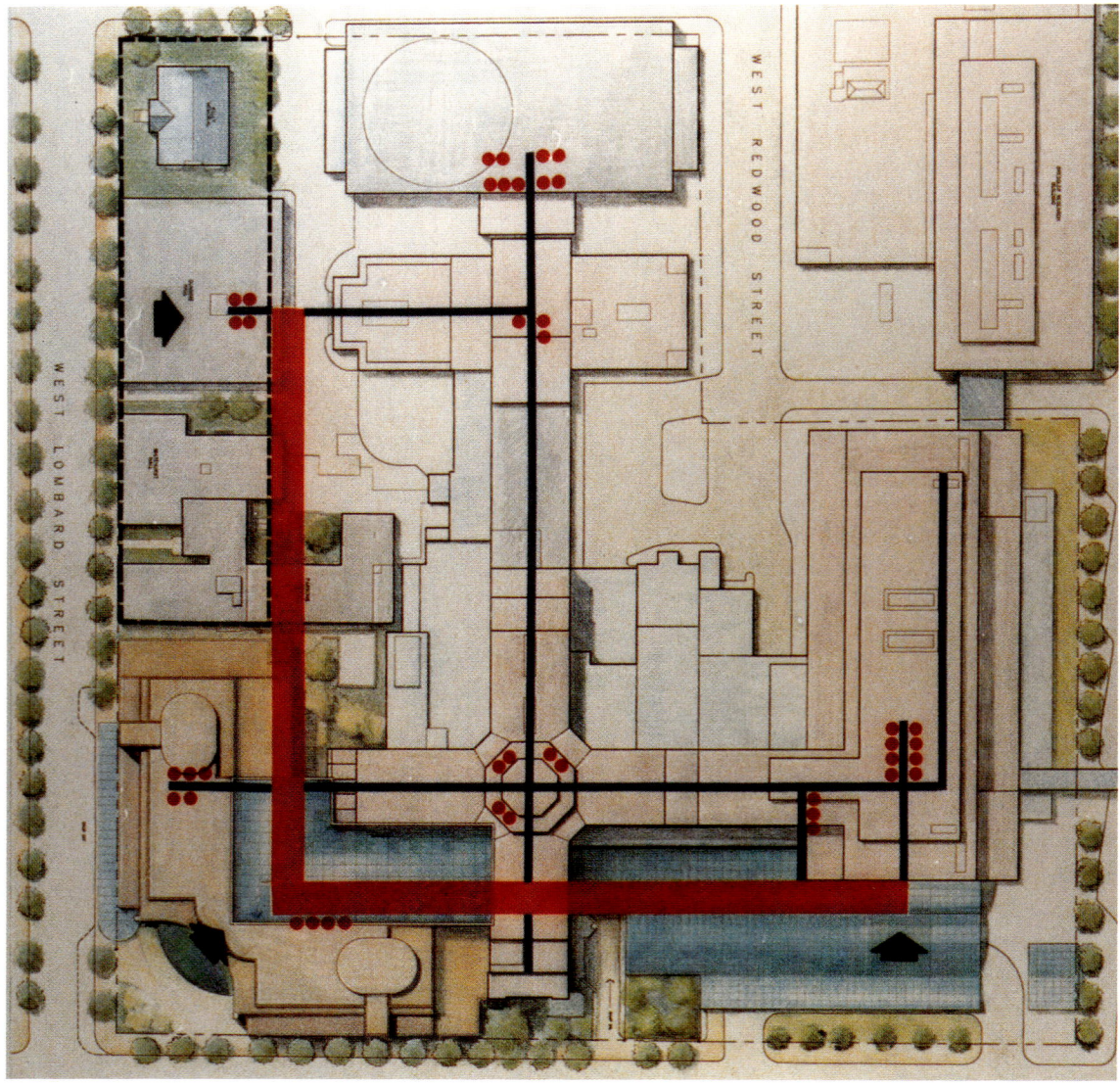

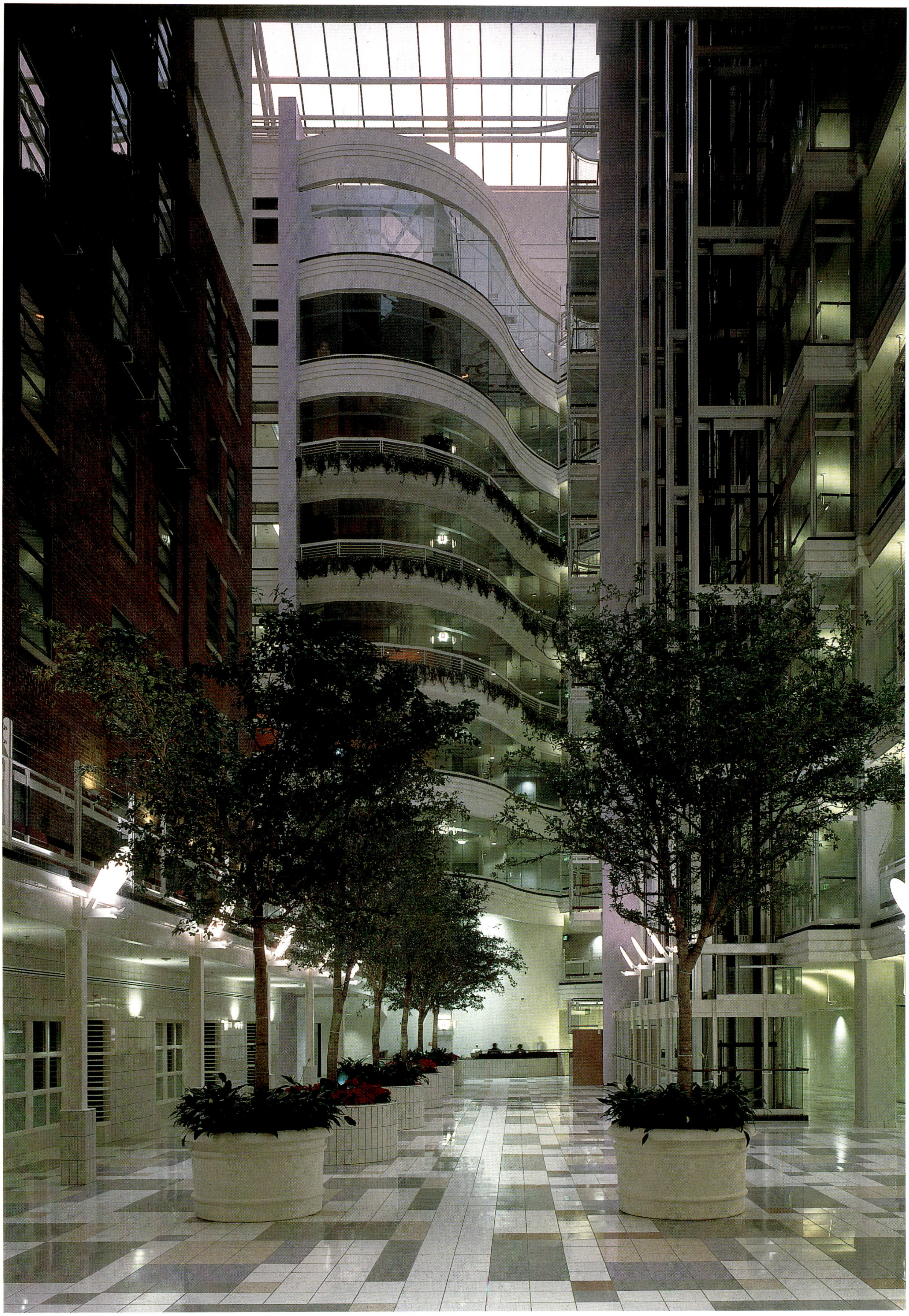

Details of the stairways around the gallery which is lit through a skylight. Opposite page, above, view of nursing station in the Critical Care Unit, below, continuation of the public circulation corridor to the north of the Gudelsky Gallery, where green has been used extensively to try and relieve the feeling of stress.

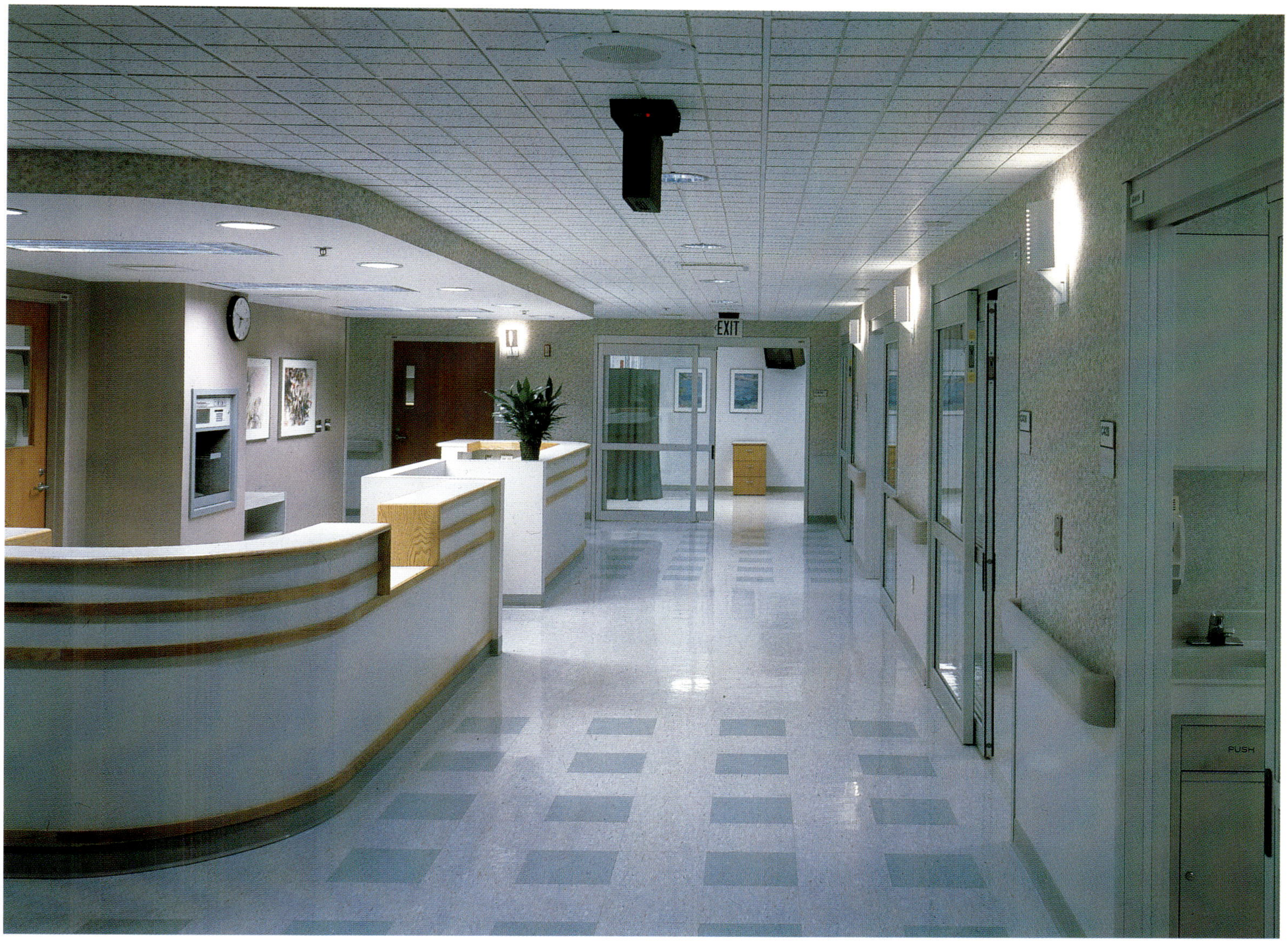
EXIT
PUSH

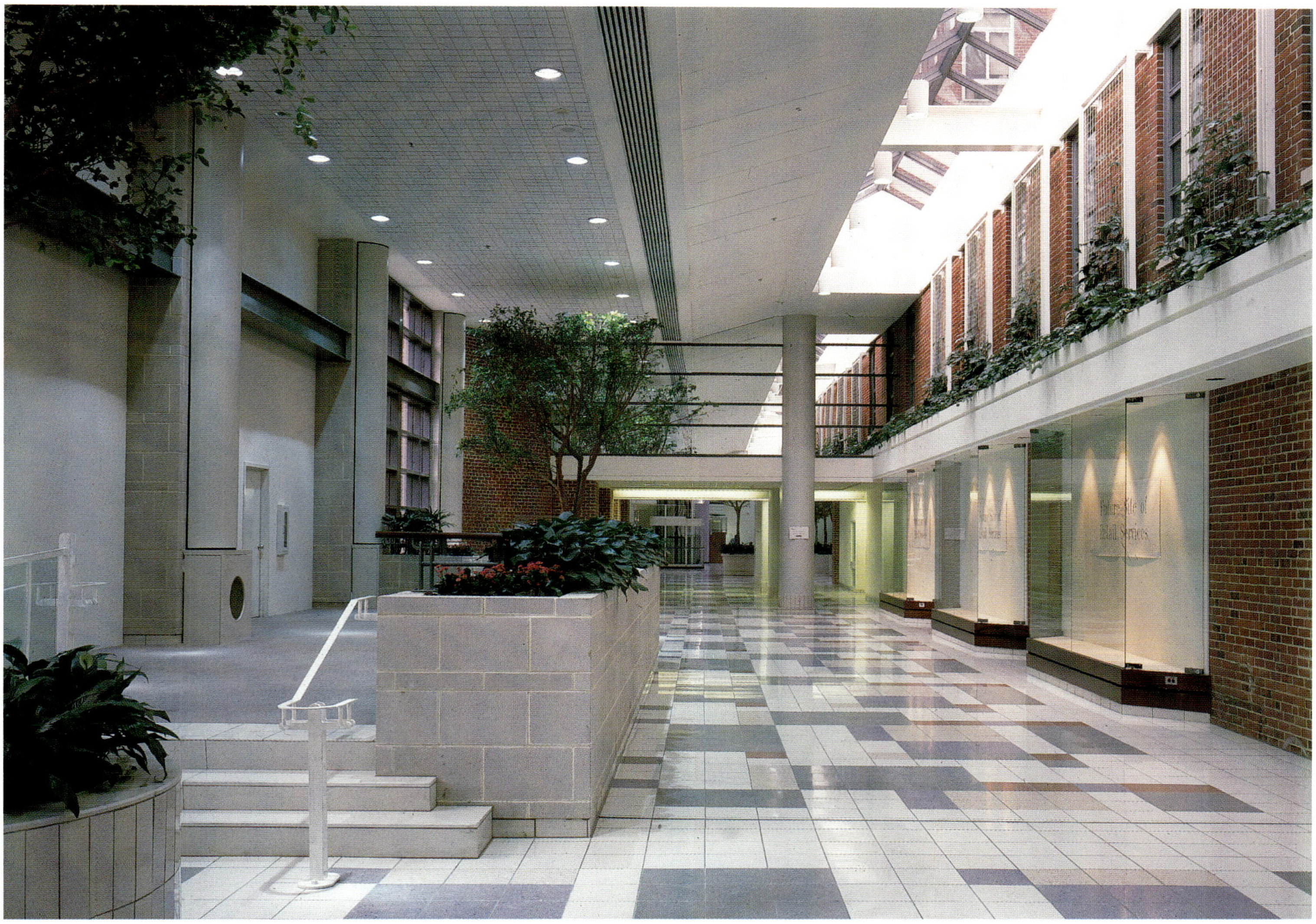

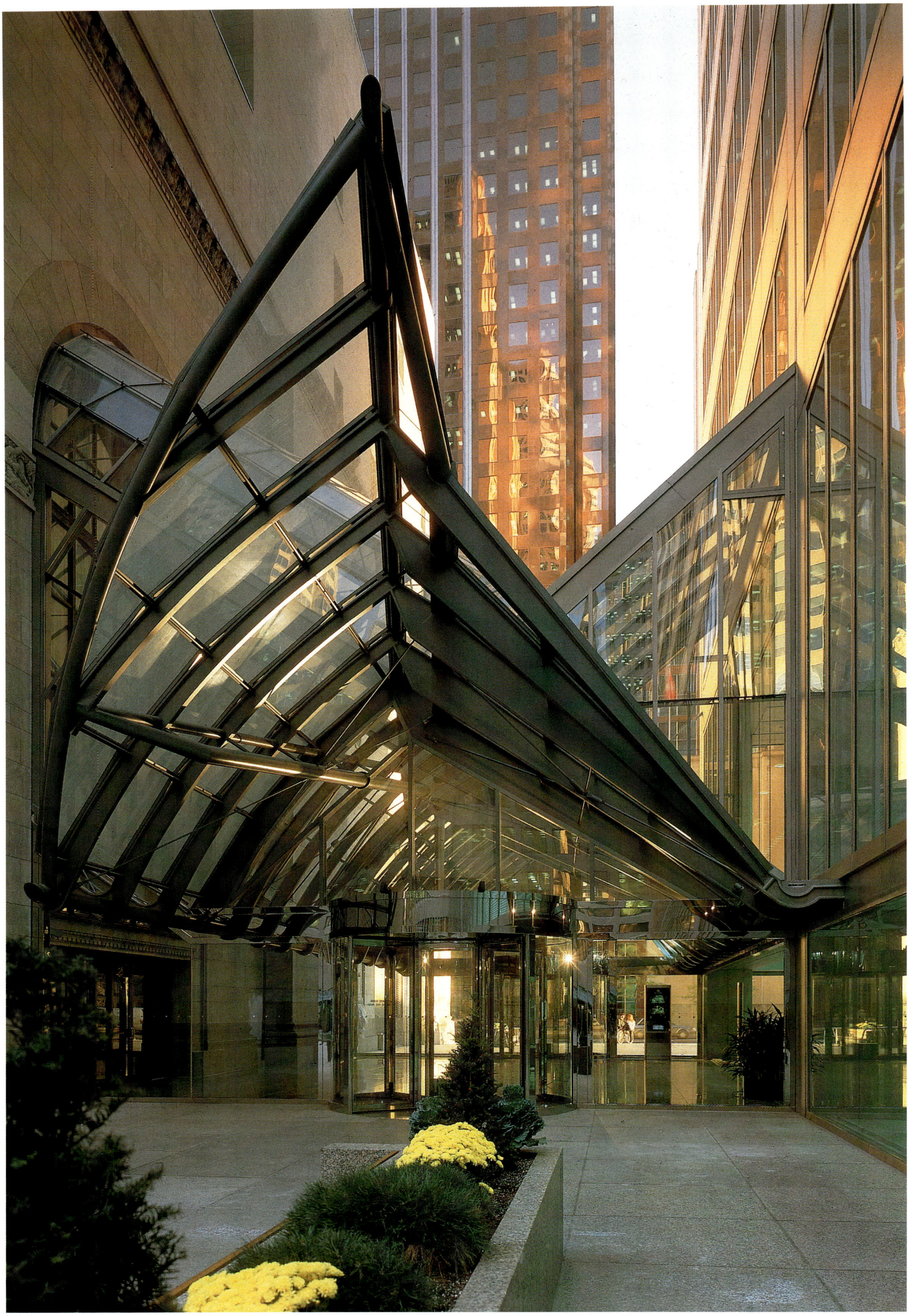

CIBC Commerce Court Renewal
Toronto, Ontario

Commerce Court is a delightful urban space which includes the historic 1930 Bank of Commerce Tower and three other buildings designed by I.M. Pei in the early Seventies. Unfortunately, despite its fabulous urban setting, the Court's appeal has been entirely visual.

The reasons for the lack of urban life within the Court were three-fold: the uninterrupted tower surfaces and their relation to each other, created strong winds, even on relatively quiet days (at times, conditions become dangerous for pedestrians); there was a limited amount of sunlight entering the Court, recently reduced even further by the construction of a tall tower to the south; and few public facilities existed within the Court which would cause pedestrians to linger there. Zeidler Roberts Partnership was entrusted with the task of ameliorating these conditions. The goal of the project was to revitalize the urban plaza, the banking area and the below-grade retail areas of this downtown Toronto architectural landmark.

Two principles were established: one was that this special place would be maintained as an urban plaza, one which would not only be attractive during the summer when the sun penetrated it, but also during Toronto's winters; the second was that all architectural adjustments would be made using the same vocabulary, so they neither interfered with the grand composition of the space, nor repeated in detail the historic 1930 building or the 1970 structures. They were to be an expression of current times, as well as harmonize with the existing building.

Wind tunnel tests determined the design solution. The gap between the north and west towers was enclosed with a glass link, as well as the opening between the east and south office buildings. A greenhouse was created in front of the east building and canopies were added at the foot of the south building, making the court useable once again by pedestrians.

The greenhouse restaurant would play a dual function, by creating seating in the plaza and by encouraging the plaza's use, even when the sun did not reach the plaza floor and only played up and down the south wall of the historic tower.

The additions needed for quieting the wind were used to provide facilities that would attract pedestrians during the summer and winter months, such as restaurants, sidewalk cafes and plaza-related retail space.

The Concourse level of the Court suffered similar neglect. Although a part of Toronto's underground walking system, it was primarily used as a subway connection by office workers. This under-use was due to a lack of entrance connections to the street system above and a lack of visual orientation. Furthermore, there was a dual mall system design which did not follow the natural pedestrian pathways. Three changes were made to improve these conditions and to integrate the Court with the existing, well-used Toronto underground system: the malls were re-oriented to follow the natural flow of pedestrians, as if they followed footsteps in the snow; the entrances into the mall were redesigned so that they could remain open 24 hours a day, instead of being closed after banking hours, as they were; and the entrances were designed to act as orientation nodes that visually connected the underground mall with the street system above, and were integrated into the pathways which connected Commerce Court with the surrounding underground system. A skylight was also introduced from which the historic building would be visible from below to create a strong and delightful orientation node for the whole system.

Interior work included 261,770-square feet of renovations and 20,700-square feet of additions, including the expansion and renovation of the retail area to 70,680-square feet and the addition of a 14,724-square foot food court. Accessibility by the handicapped and the general public was improved by making changes to the traffic patterns and by introducing new pedestrian tunnel connections. The firm also renovated the 60,000-square foot flagship branch of the Canadian Imperial Bank of Commerce (CIBC), as an integral part of the project. The fractal geometry of the new design was used to integrate the 1930 and the 1970 building forms.

Bottom left, plan of the concourse level before and, right, after the project was completed. Above, left, the court level before and, right, after completion. Opposite page, the new glass canopy marking the entrance from Wellington Street into the underground mall.

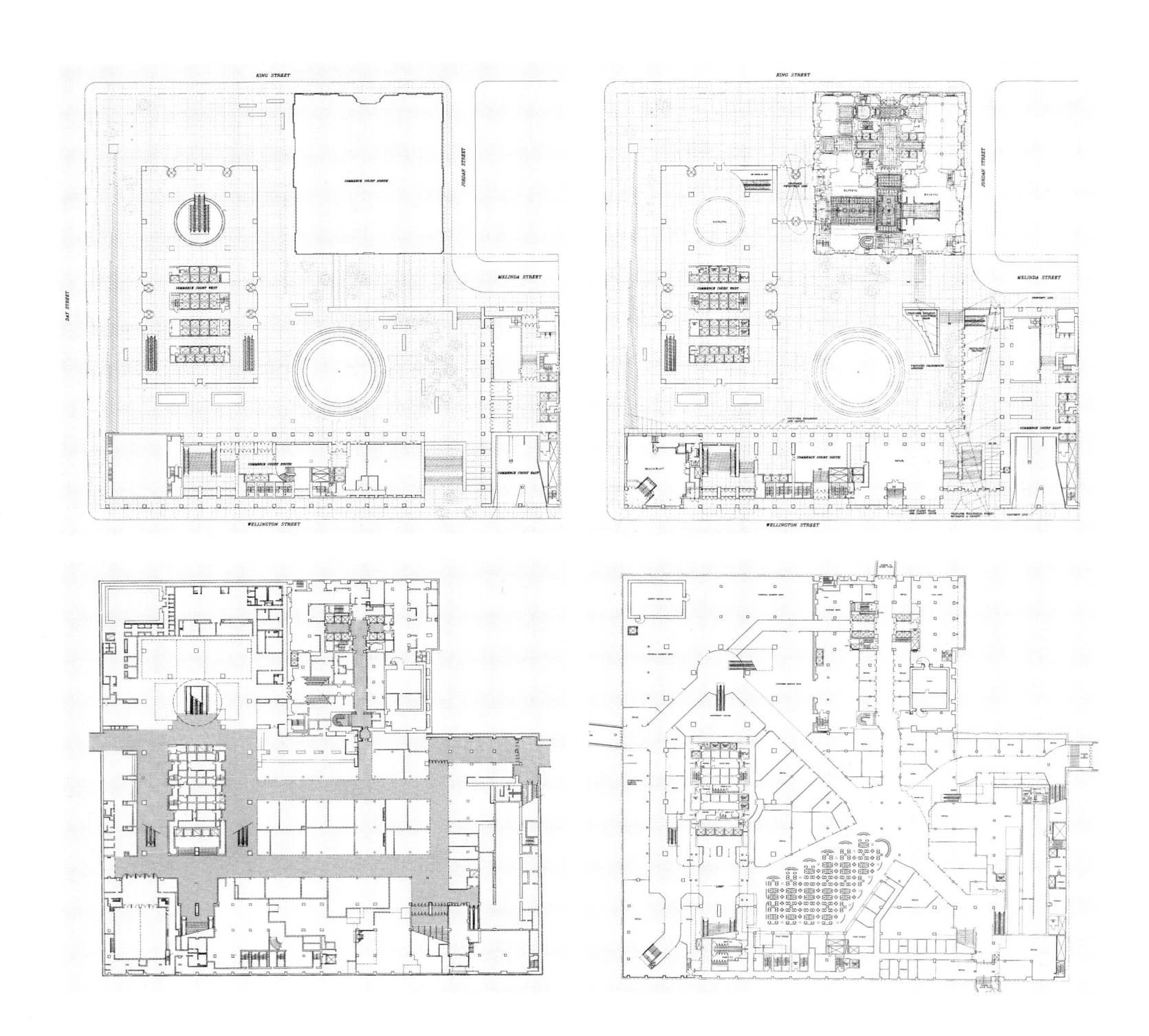

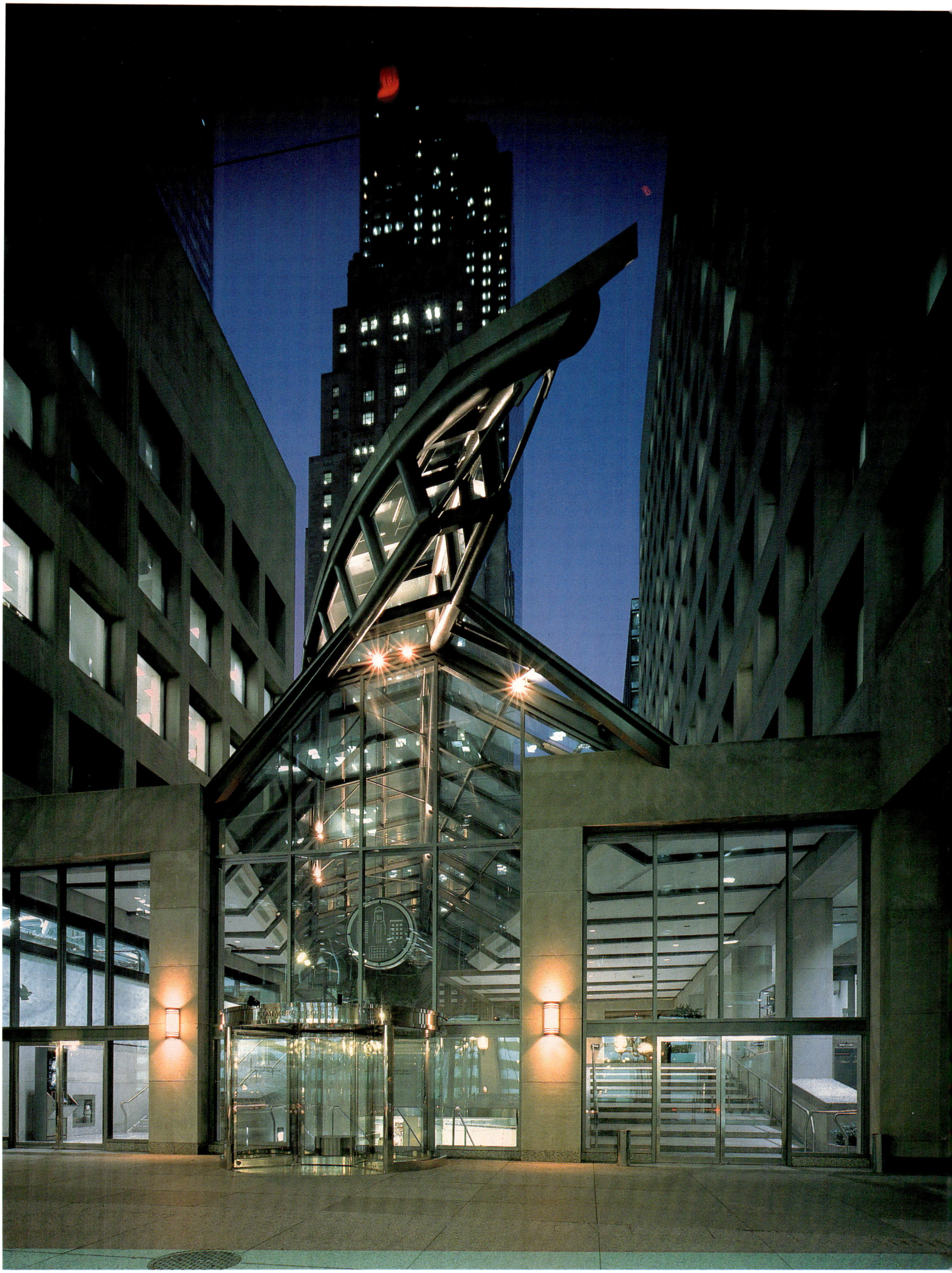

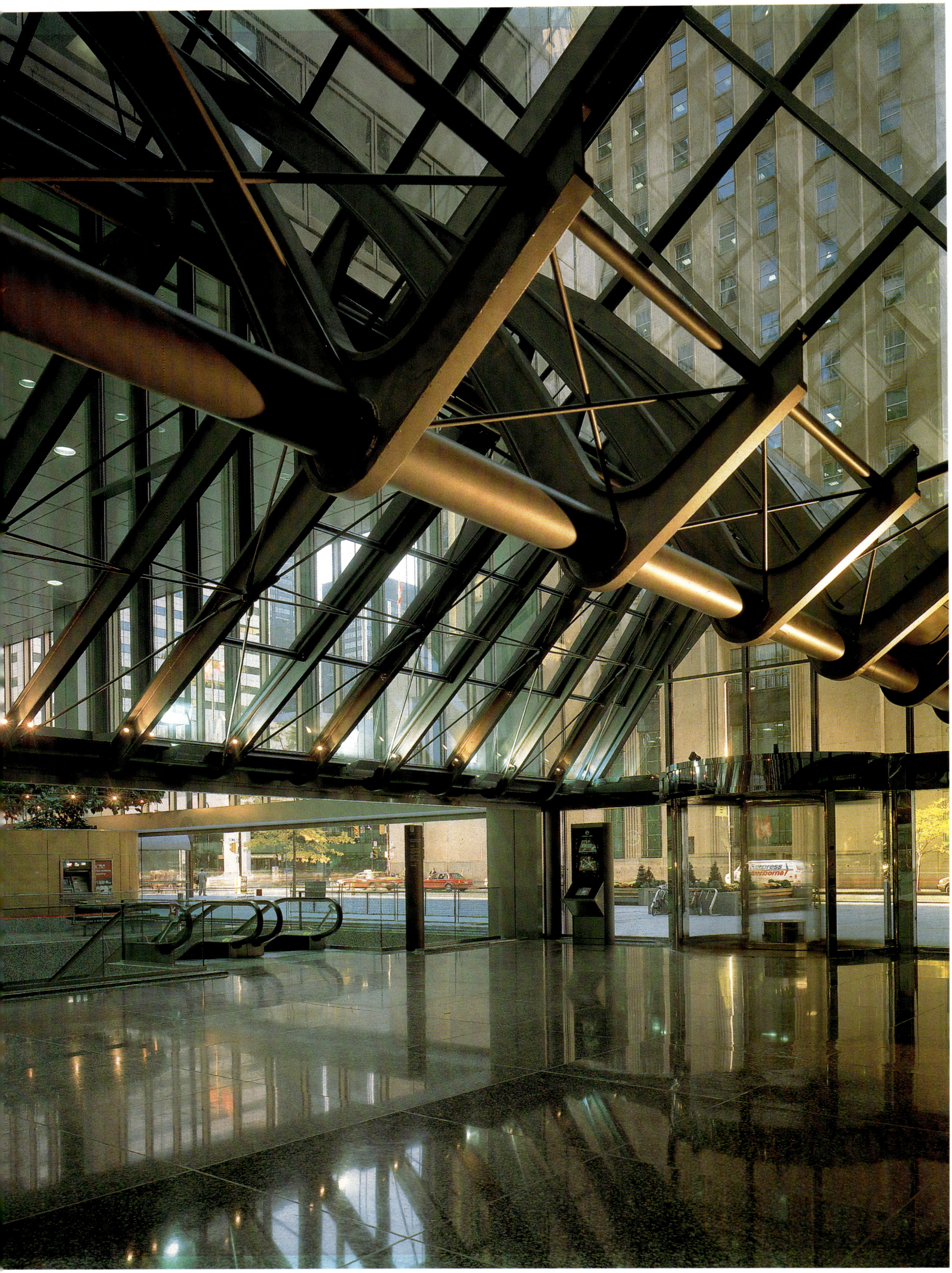

Opposite page, the entrance from King Street into the underground mall and the court. This page, below, the "wind break" connecting the court with the King Street entrance. Top view from the court into Bay Street.

69

Opposite page, the view from the underground mall toward Wellington Street, which created an integration of the street system with Toronto's underground pedestrian system. This page, the renovated banking hall for automated banking.

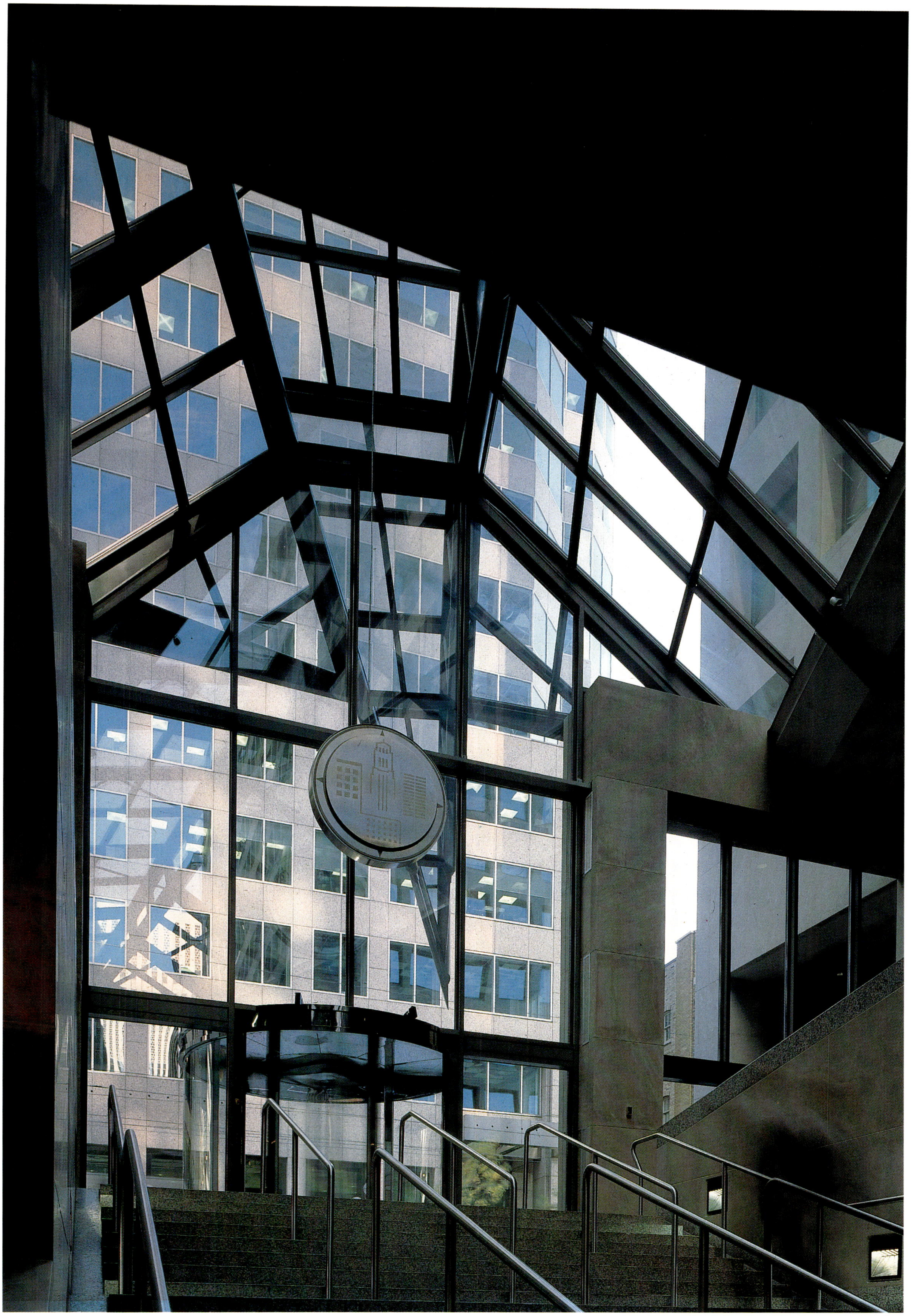

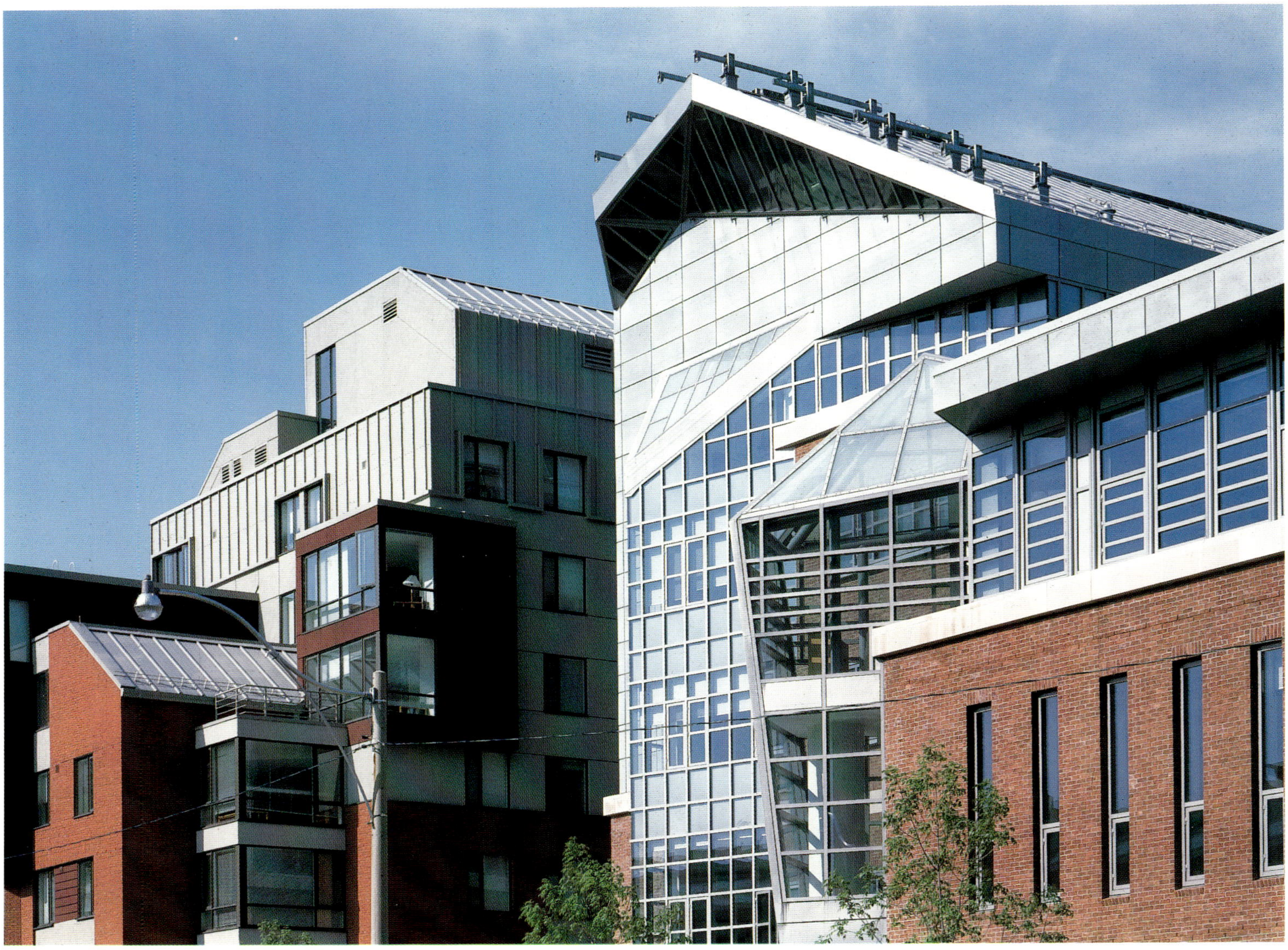

University of Toronto
Joseph L. Rotman Centre for Management
Toronto, Ontario

The new home of the Faculty of Management at the University of Toronto expresses both the tradition and history of the university campus and that of St. George Street.

An institution with such diverse needs, required a number of individual spaces that would fulfill these requirements: classrooms, a library, study areas, faculty offices, and, of course, interactive social facilities. All the facilities needed to relate to each other in a physical sense (classrooms that could be easily reached), but also needed to reflect the spirit of the school and its approach to education.

The existing school was a typical expression of an outdated concept of education that denied the need for a spiritual response. Examples were the nondescript entrances, the labyrinth of corridors, stairs and elevators which lead to individual teaching spaces, classrooms, a library, and faculty offices.. Upon entering a building, one should be aware of its spirit and function and of its diverse activities. An educational building should open up to you immediately, clearly displaying the educational facilities and the various didactic activities on the first three levels. The entrances to the classrooms should be visible and the balconies surrounding the space should make movement between the classrooms, student facilities and study spaces easier. Instant identification of the library should invite the student to use it.

The central space, or the atrium in the building is in fact, the student lounge/locker room area used in a unique way. The lockers are concealed in cubicles, accessible from behind, but not visible from the atrium. The space itself can be transformed into a lounge for everyday use, which encourages the interchange of ideas between students and faculty. Imaginative interior landscaping gives this place an intimacy that conceals crowds as well as reveals them. In other words, the space looks active with just a few students in it, but is able to contain a large number of people without feeling crowded. In addition to lounge seating, the atrium contains a number of small café-style tables and a servery. The space is flexible and can be used for a number of student activities, ranging from large group banquets to lectures and school assemblies.

Another factor to consider when designing educational facilities is how the school should be represented on the outside. It is essential that while expressing its meaning, the building also fits into its urban context, as a member of the community.

These two interior and exterior factors cannot be resolved in isolation as they are intrinsically related to each other and a resolution must be found that responds to both.

The urban conditions of St. George Street created a number of principles established by its Victorian character which needed to be reflected in the new building: the break-up into a number of seemingly separate buildings, rather than one large building whose massing would be out of scale with the rest of the street; respect for the materials that were predominantly used: reddish brick, whitish limestone and gray roofing materials; a harmonious composition of architectural elements: a variety of window expressions, protrusions of bay windows, a tripartite stacking of materials (stone base, brick body and different gable material), and an adherence to these principles to create a coherent urban setting that had previously been lacking, while still allowing for new elements to be introduced. A new element which was introduced was the Centre for Management with its post-industrial society mission to educate a new generation of students capable of dealing with the complex issues of management in a changing world. The classic order expressed in the Euclidean geometry of the Victorian architecture only partially expresses this. A new fractal geometry, the understanding of chaos as a different but extremely complex order, has been introduced. Thus, a projection of two orders is expressed in the new facade. Its base is the Euclidean geometry of a Victorian building with its small scale massing, materials and complexity of architectural expression. Overlaid on this is the vision of a new order of global economy, reaching beyond the confines of the campus, expressed by fractal geometry, which adds a new visual dimension to the building. All these are tightly interwoven into the urban presence in a visual and functional way. The building opens onto the street and the surrounding pedestrian walkways from which the classrooms, offices and study spaces are visible, yet the building respects the historical quadrangle around which the school activities are focused. This creates an urban event accessible from all sides in varying ways, visible from the street, with passages through its gateways in the university tradition.

From bottom of page up, plans of the first, second and third floors. Opposite page, top, general view and view of the entrance to the complex that evokes the Victorian-style urban surroundings through its intricate fractal facade. Bottom, Innis College, also designed by ZRP/A with the Rotman Centre at the end maintaining the character of St. George Street.

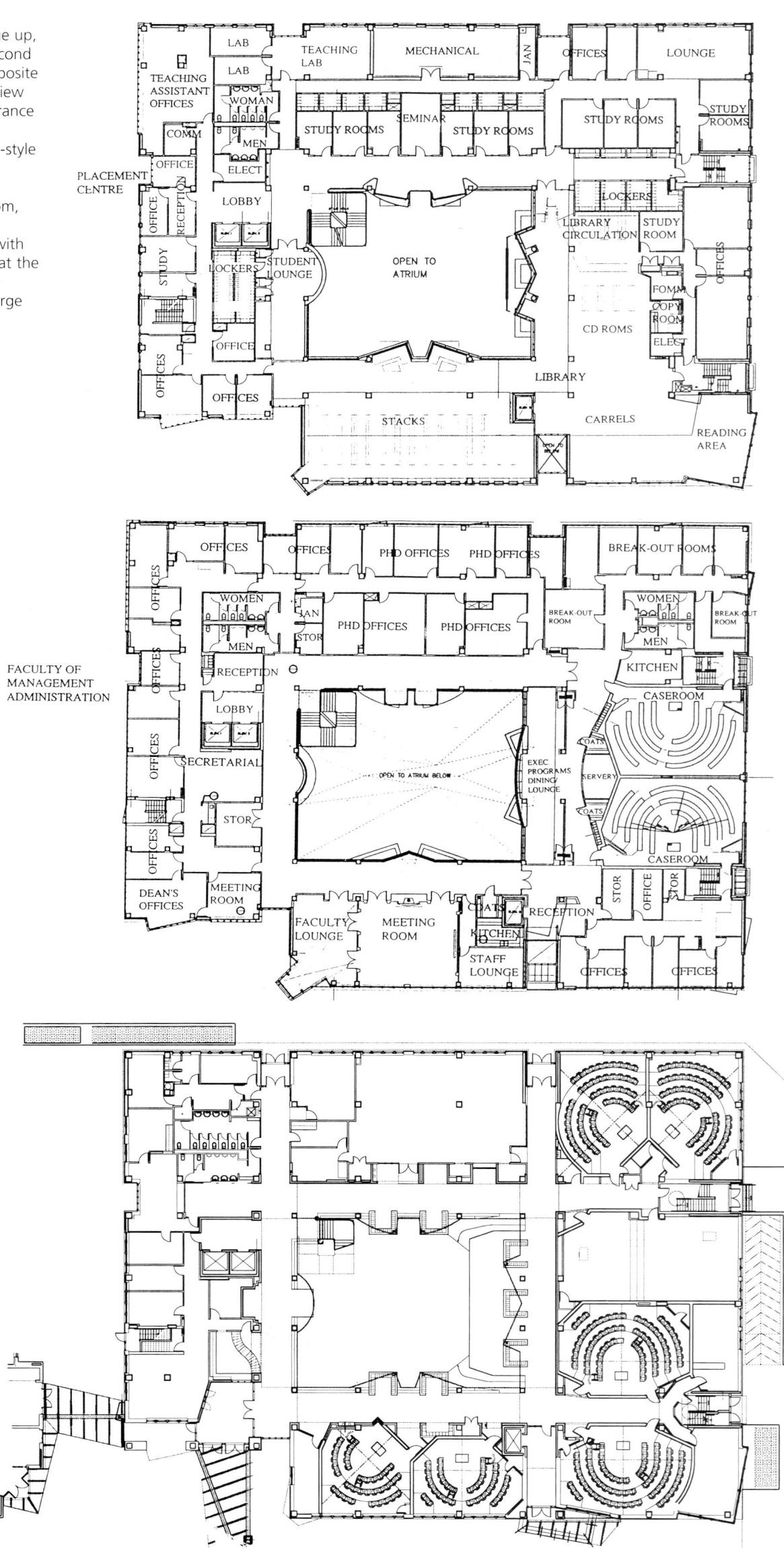

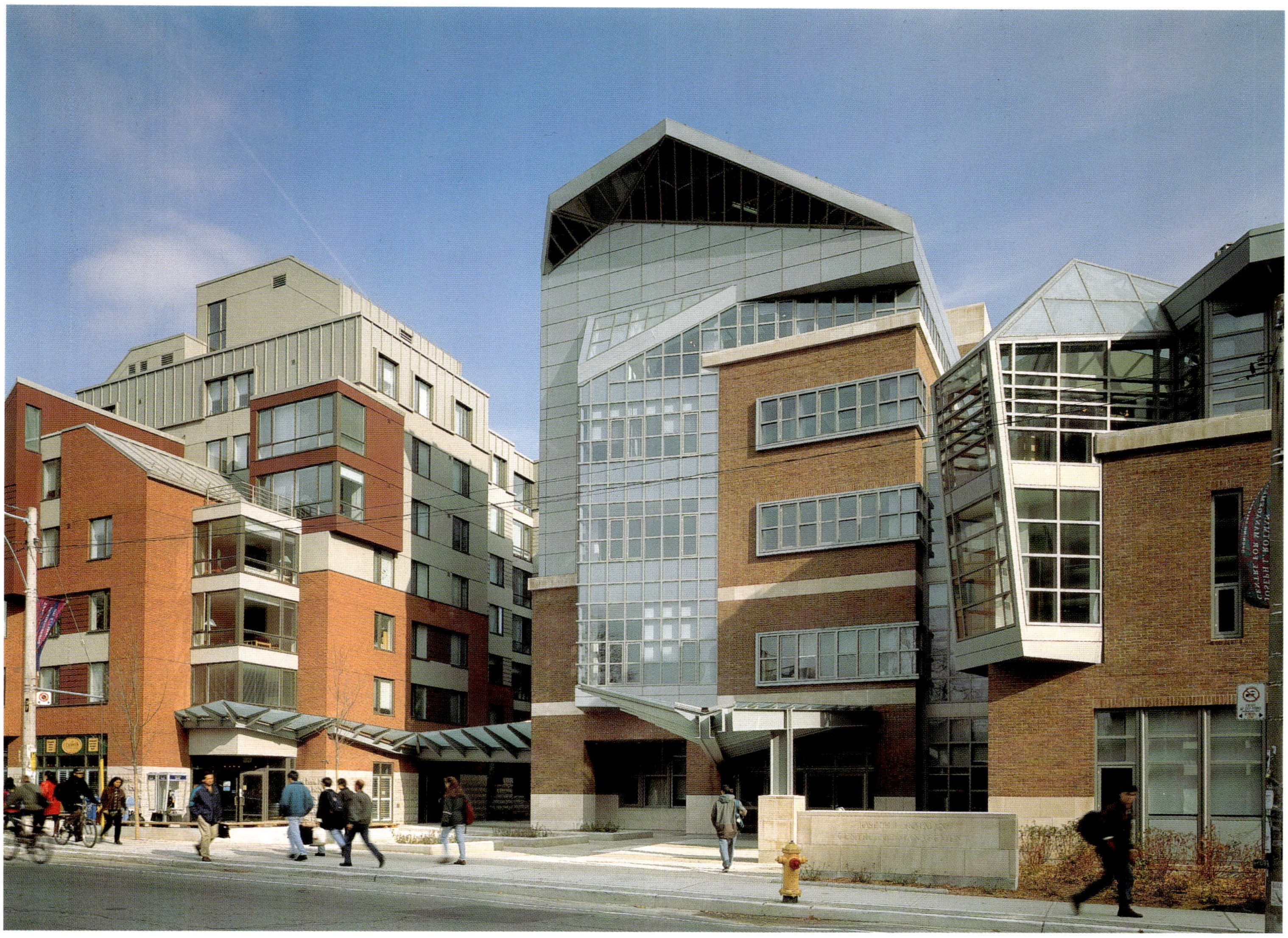

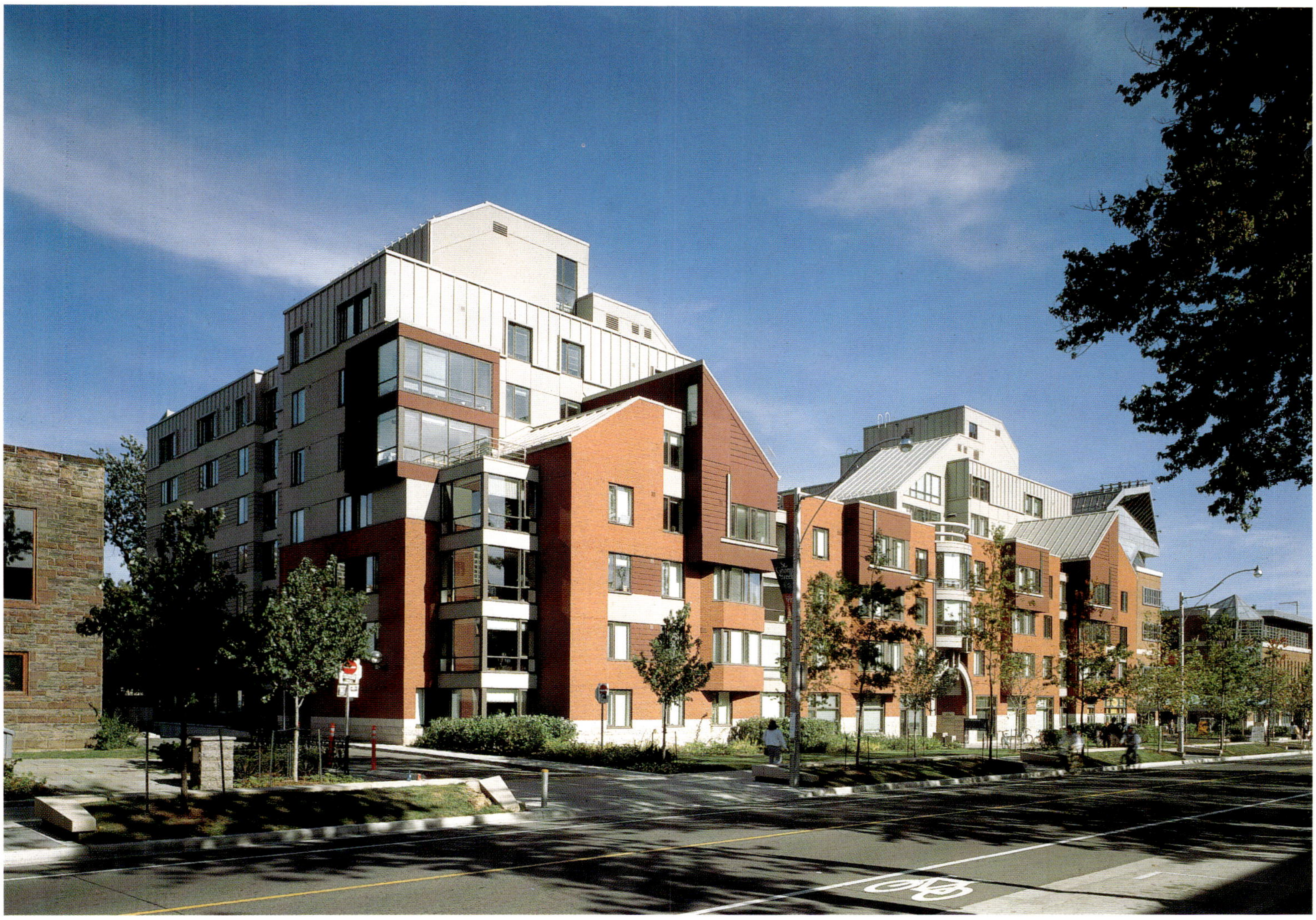

The glass gallery to the library seen from the central lobby. Opposite page, the central lobby naturally lit through a skylight cutting through the roof; notice to the back of a locker cubicle.

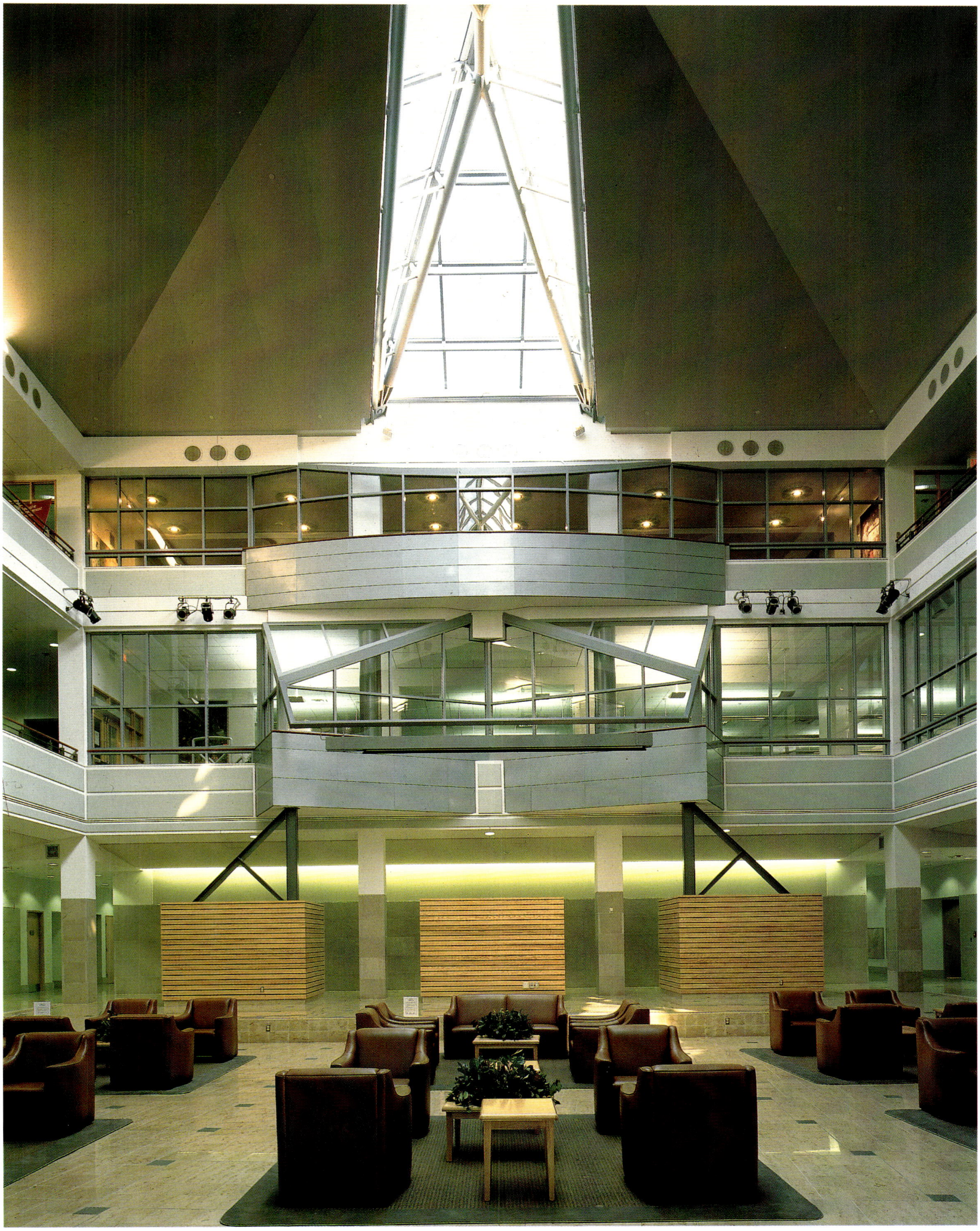

One of the top-floor panoramic lounges. Bottom, one of the classrooms. Opposite page, view of the entrance, whose glass surfaces create a sense of invitation.

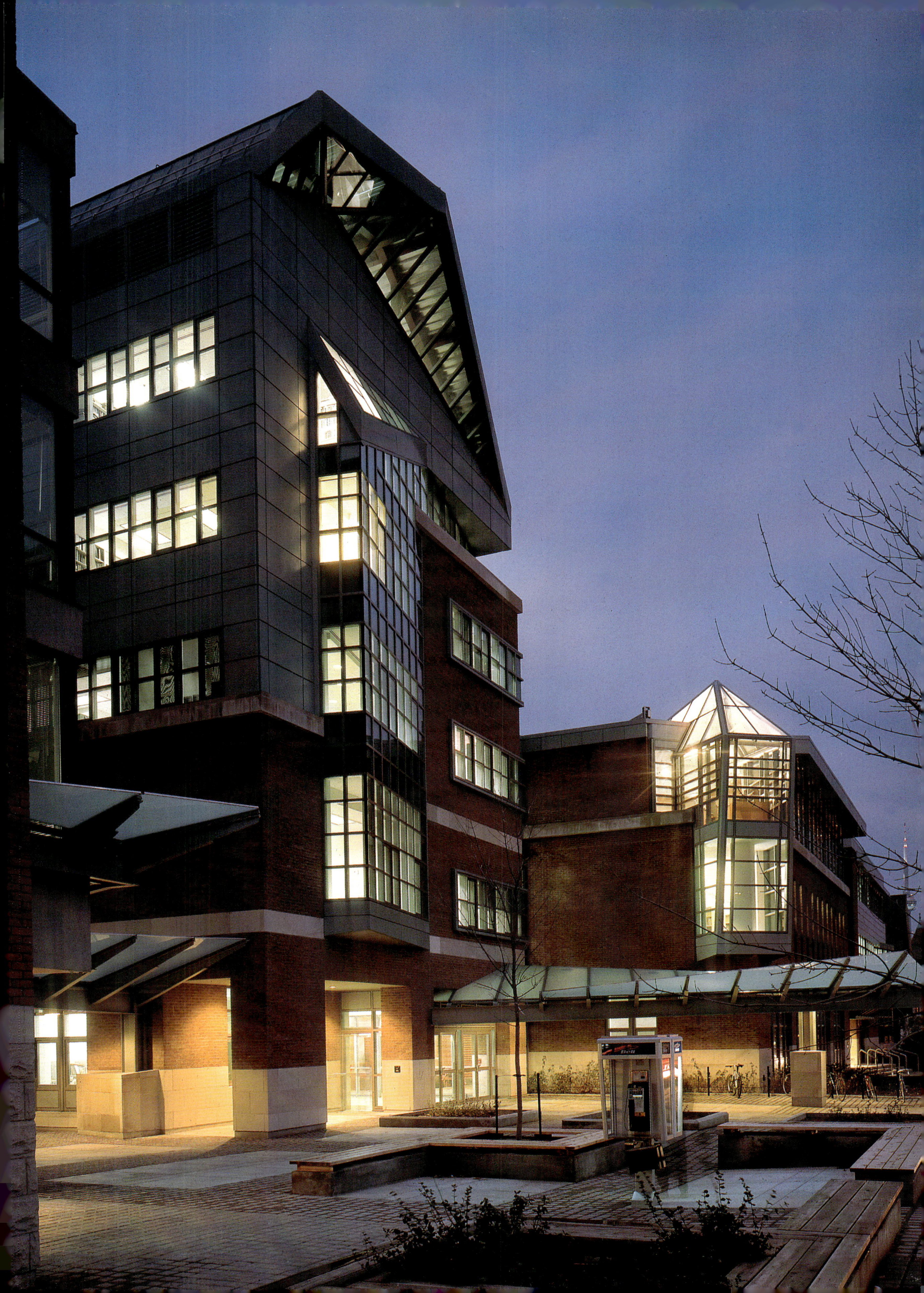

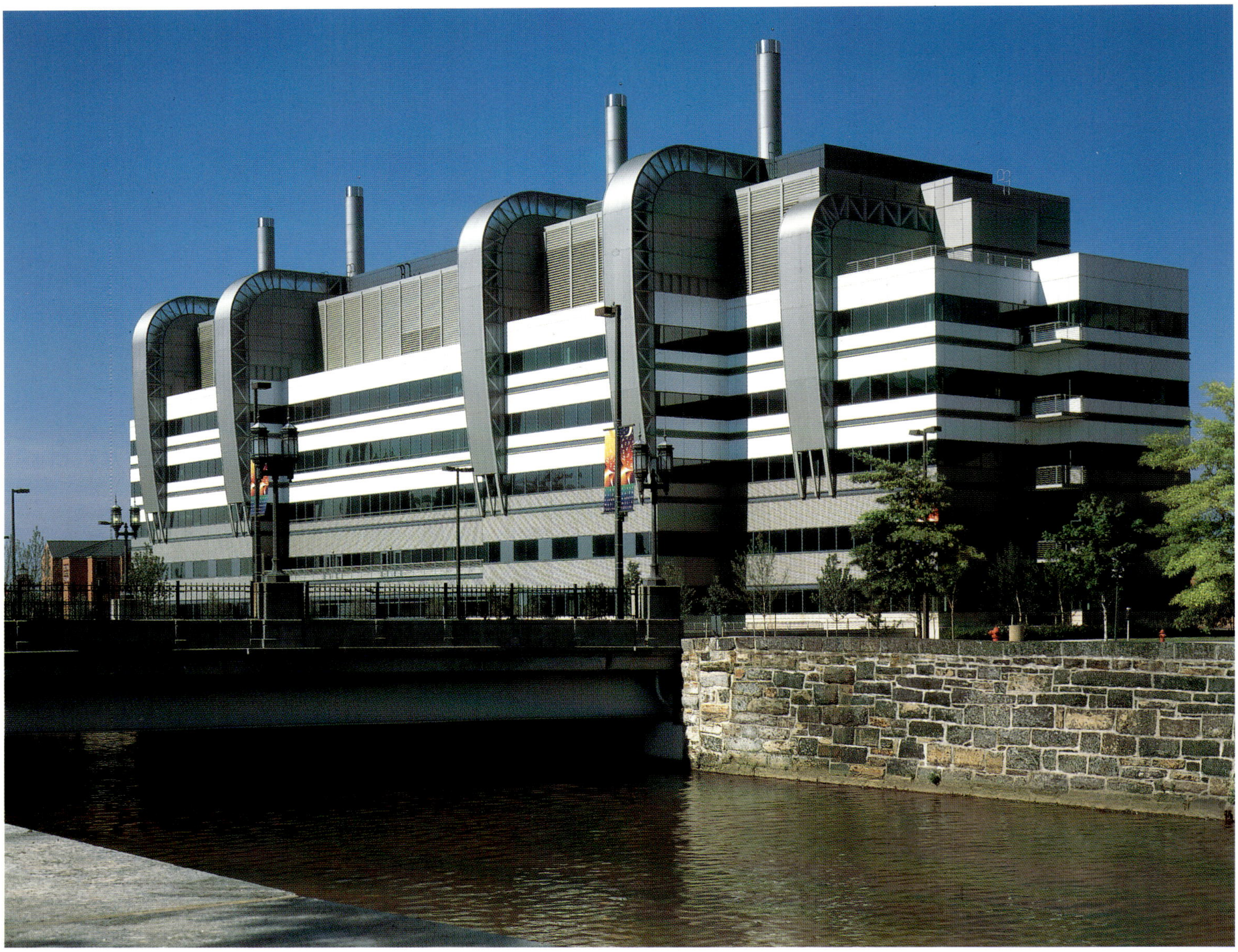

Columbus Centre of Marine Research and Exploration

Baltimore, Maryland

The Columbus Centre houses the University of Maryland's new Marine Research and Exploration Centre. The urban setting, in the middle of a vibrant tourist area, places the scientific community purposely on public display. Two contradictory functions, the isolated nature of scientific research versus an open approach to the public, presented challenges to the design. The massing and placement of the building on the pier followed a simple strategy: to complement the existing buildings in the neighbourhood such as the Aquarium, the Power Plant and the old warehouses which have been converted into office space. By not aligning the building to the pier edge, the designers not only acknowledged the change in the city grid at this point, but also achieved better exposure to the water opposite the Power Plant. Moreover, the resultant wedge between the building and the promenade at the water's edge created space for a unique landscape feature - the Marsh.

Located on Piers 5 and 6 of Baltimore's Inner Harbor, the 260,200-square foot Centre comprises four interrelated research and educational components. The research component consists of the University of Maryland's Centre of Marine Biotechnology, which is a unit of the Maryland Biotechnology Institute, and the Food and Drug Administration's National Seafood Safety Centre (a total of 133,400-square feet of laboratory space). The two educational components are the Science and Technology Education Centre and The Hall of Exploration exhibit area. The research component is organized in a rational pattern that not only fulfills its functional demands, but also creates an environment that encourages interaction between scientific staff (e.g. lab clusters, vertically integrated lounges, etc.). The exhibition area is located within a fabric-enclosed atrium. The desired dialogue of the interior space with the exterior of the building is achieved by means of a glazed wall which runs along the atrium. Exhibitions are organized on terrace-like, stepped platforms.

Most important in the design was the interface between the "public" and "private" segments of the project. Windows into the laboratories became the necessary visual link between the scientist and the public. In the middle of the block, vertically stacked lounges relate to each other and to the exhibition level. Likewise, the elevators used by the scientists are exposed, animating the space. The character of the diffused light, in combination with the direct sunlight filtering in through the suspended skylights, contributes to the special character of the main exhibition space.

The exhibition design needs to be able to deal with diverse subject matters (i.e., the natural, visible part, as well as with the abstract character of molecular biotechnology). To bridge this huge territory, the space was designed as a series of events, interactive in character and placed in a colourful environment. This space is primarily situated on the second floor, with the exhibitions and entry functions on the ground floor, while the third floor is devoted to traveling exhibitions, refreshment areas, and to relaxation.

The landscaped wedge extends the theme of the exhibit to the outdoors. Designed as a tidal marsh one can hear the rhythm of the flooding and draining. Its flora resembles that of Chesapeake Bay. Suspended wood bridges stretching across the Marsh double as observation walkways.

The choice of materials reflects the design philosophy. The laboratory building uses a combination of metal cladding and glass strip windows. The exhibition atrium is created by a glazed perimeter curtain wall and a fabric roof with the organic form of four skylights. The fabric roof is stretched through the hydraulic columns which support the glass skylights. The metal cladding uses a rhythm of corrugated metal bands with inset gray-blue "C" channels. White painted panels occur towards the top of the facade; while corrugated metal clads the penthouse. Special attention was given to the design of the laboratory service shafts. They are glazed on two sides and are faced with curved corrugated metal. The purpose of this is to highlight the technical system of the project. The Centre was an attempt to design a new building type, perhaps with an unorthodox result.

From bottom of page up, plans of the ground floor, first floor and second floor.

1. Centre of Marine Biotechnology
2. Hall of Exploration
3. Science and Technology Education Centre
4. Food and Drug Administration
5. Administration

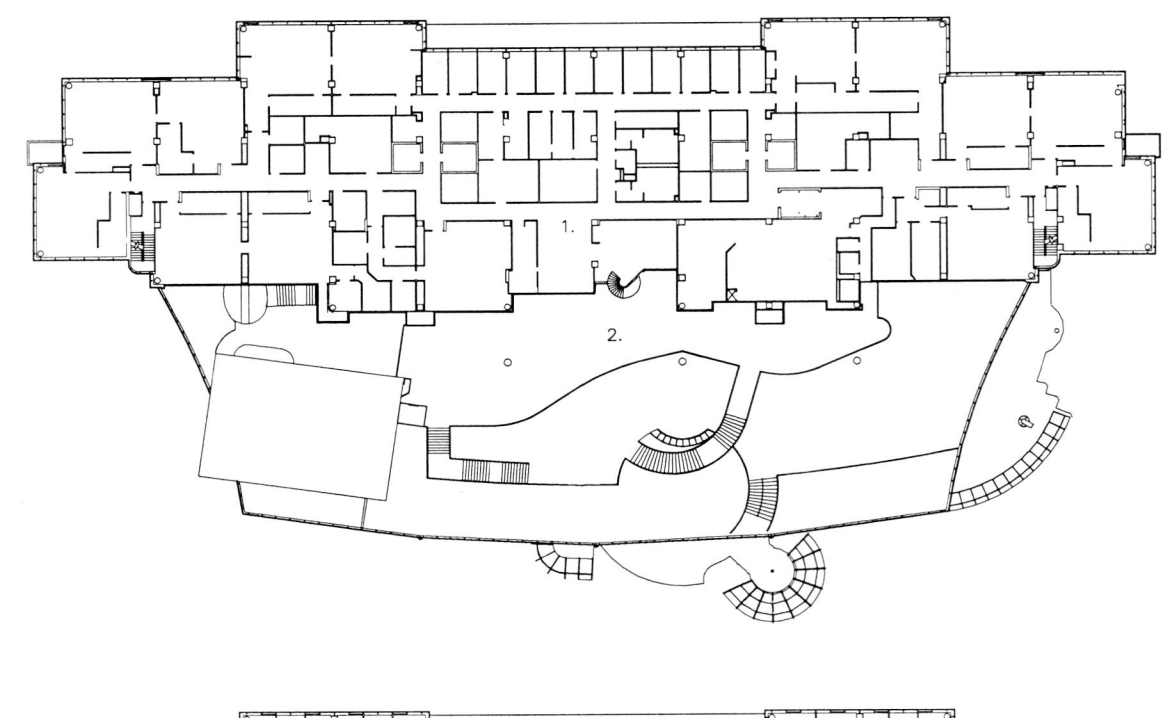

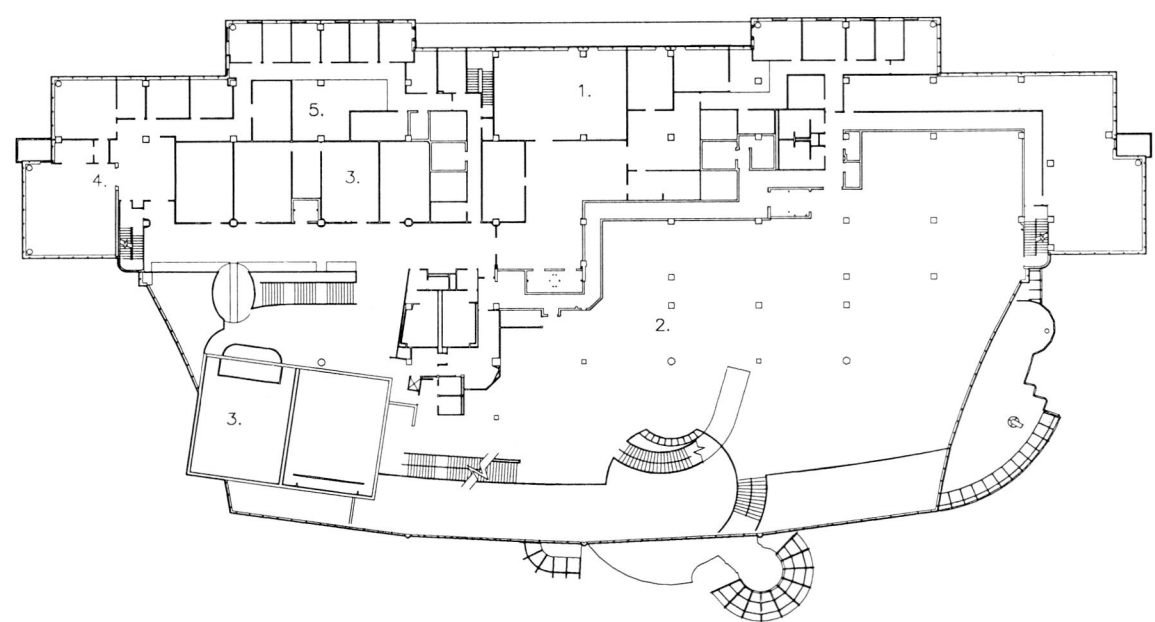

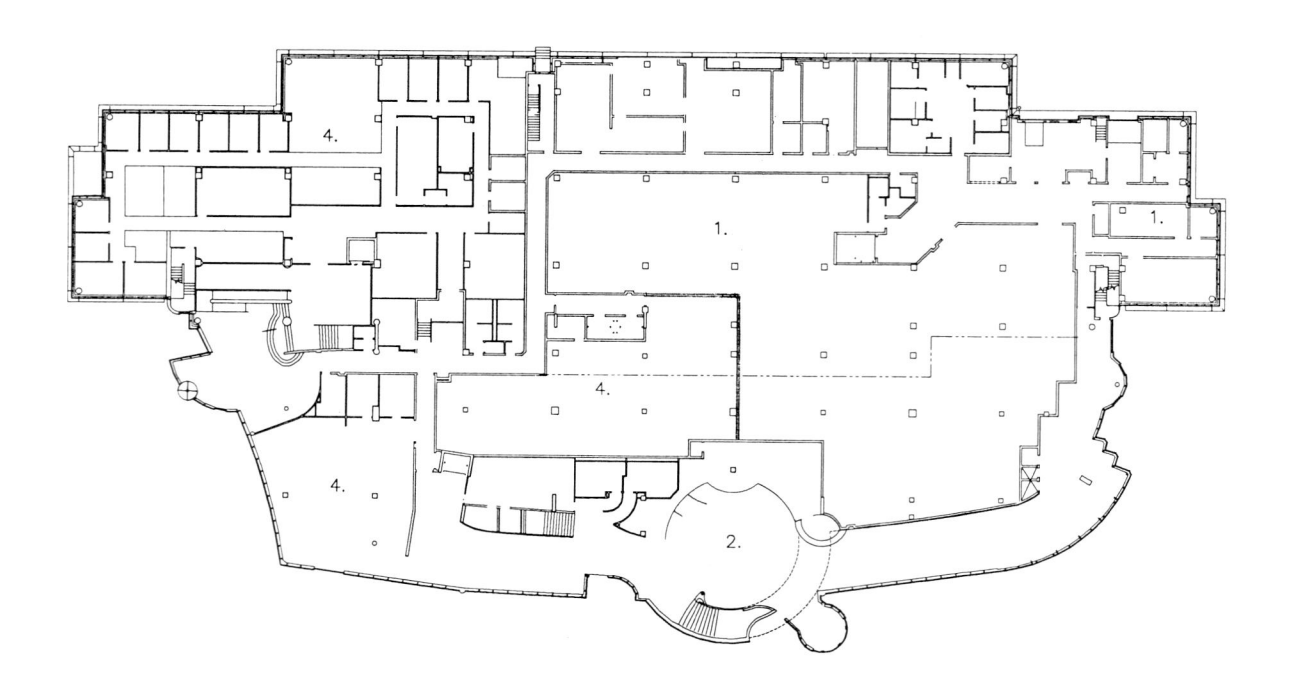

Longitudinal section and, bottom, nighttime view of the west facade featuring a large tensile structure covering the Centre's exhibition and education facilities.

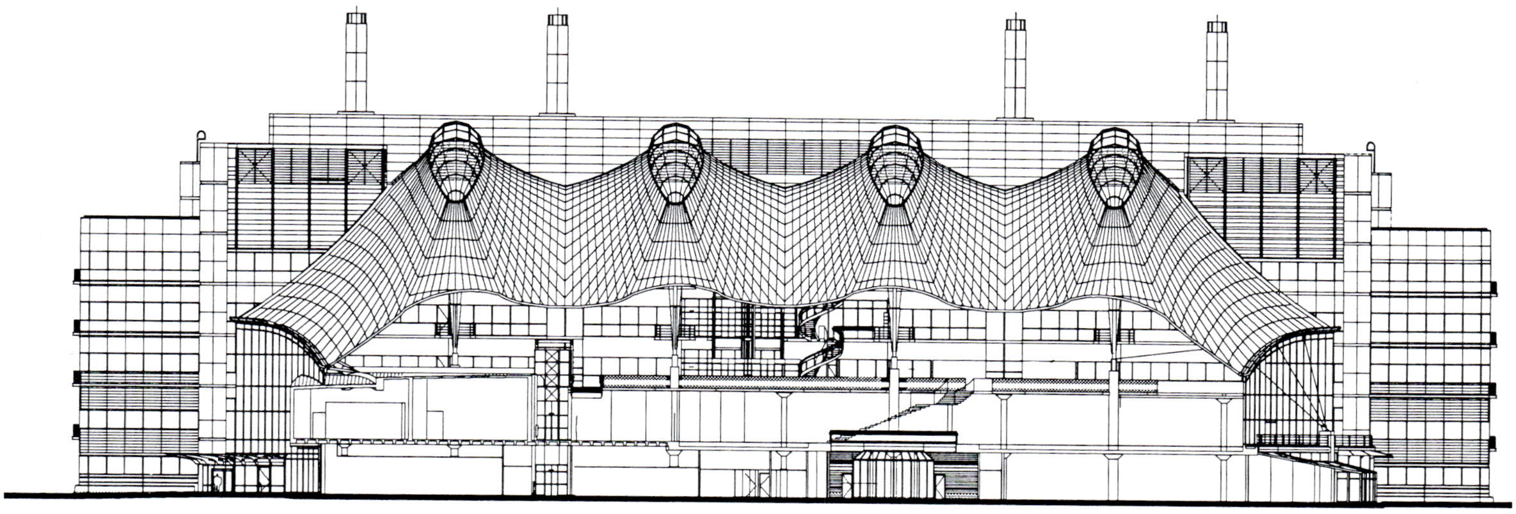

83

Details of the entrance to the Hall of Exploration overlooking Piers 5 and 6 of Baltimore's Inner Harbor.

The exhibition space inside the tensile structure is arranged in a series of terraces affording a view into the research laboratories.

Top, main entrance into research lab. Bottom, details of the stairways linking the various levels of the research laboratories with a view into the exhibition space.

The ground floor entrance into the exhibition space at the rear, research laboratories.

DNA
CONTRIBUTORS
Contributors
Cool TOOLS
Blue PLANET
Welcome to COLUMBUS CENTER'S Hall of Exploration
Information
Coat Check

Princess Margaret Hospital

Ontario Cancer Institute Princess Margaret Hospital

Toronto, Ontario

Founded in 1958 in Toronto, the Ontario Cancer Institute/Princess Margaret Hospital is recognized internationally for its outstanding achievements in the treatment and research of cancer.

With its facilities outdated and insufficient, it was decided to relocate the new hospital building beside Mount Sinai Hospital, close to the University of Toronto's hospitals and main campus. This proximity would promote better communication among staff, teachers and students and provide oncology patients with improved treatment as a result of interdisciplinary teamwork.

The new 860,000-square foot institution was relocated to a constrained 61,400-square foot urban site which included two historically significant buildings. The first is an 18-storey office building built in the 1930's, which had been retained and partially renovated for the hospital's use. The six-storey facade of a 1915 building was also incorporated into the new structure, but only its facade was retained as the interior had been destroyed in a previous renovation. The new facilities were therefore restricted to a site of only 42,000-square feet.

These site restrictions, combined with the required functional area, dictated a high-rise building solution. Furthermore, functional adjacencies with Mount Sinai Hospital had to be achieved as these two institutions were to share various facilities.

To achieve floor plates large enough to suit these functional demands and to leave Murray Street open for traffic, the upper floors were cantilevered 20-feet over the street.

The design objectives were: to create a well functioning hospital in which related functions were connected as closely as possible to each other, as well as to the front entrances; to create a clear orientation system that avoided unnecessary traffic and achieved separation of public, inpatient and material movement; to locate the two public elevator banks for inpatients and outpatients in the visible centre of the entrance area; to place research areas not as an appendix, but as a focus within the hospital; to create a quiet and nearly pastoral setting for the inpatient units within the hospital; to make the hospital easily accessible from University Avenue, the subway station and Murray Street, to have all entrances focusing on the vertical transportation nodes; and finally, to create a positive emotional atmosphere within the hospital.

The two historic buildings on University Avenue (numbers 610 and 620) totally occupied the frontage on this street. Because they had to be preserved, they created a particular challenge in the design. The hospital board wanted a prominent entrance from University Avenue, while the historical board wanted visibility of the east and south facades of 620 University Avenue, and retention of the whole structure.

To maintain the visual presence of the historic 1930's building, the hospital's east facade was set back behind the facade of the 1915 building. The design of the new building, however, continues the strong plasticity of this facade. A skylight cuts into the last window of the 1915 facade, connecting the old and the new, and transfers the historicism of the old facade into an equally strong but contemporary expression, while creating a symbiosis among the three architecturally adjacent facades: the historicism of the 1915 facade; the Art Deco 1930 building; and the Modern facade of Mount Sinai. The north, east and south facades of the hospital that enclose the historic structures harmonize with the surrounding urban texture in form and material through the use of stone, glass and metal.

The hospital has been organized vertically around two atria and divided into four sectors stacked on top of each other.

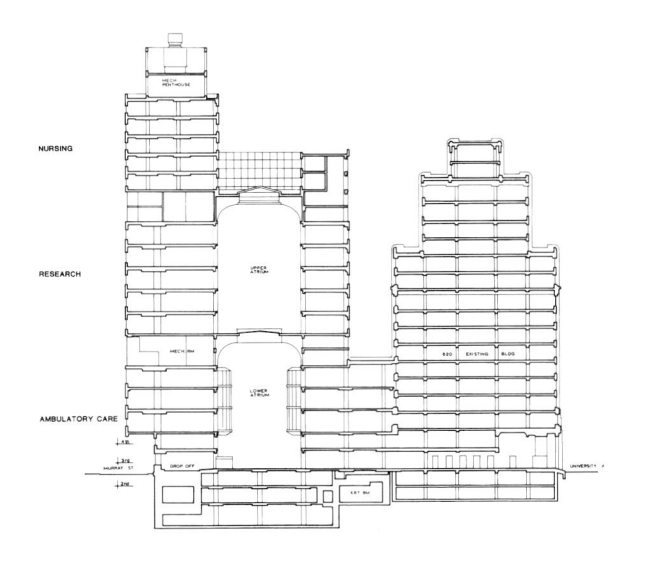

From bottom of page up, plans of the below ground floor, the eighth floor (research) and 17th floor (in-patient floor). Previous page, east-west section.
Opposite page, the facade along Murray Street.

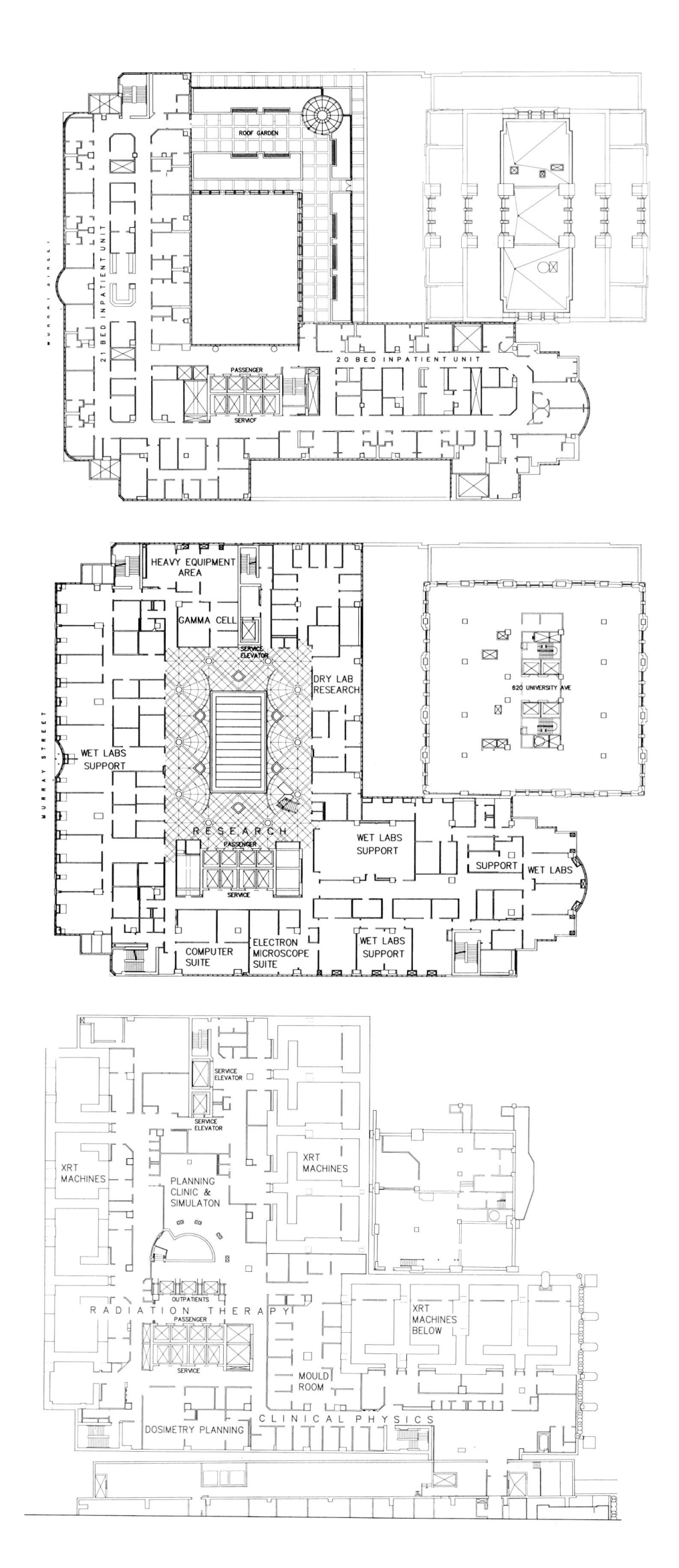

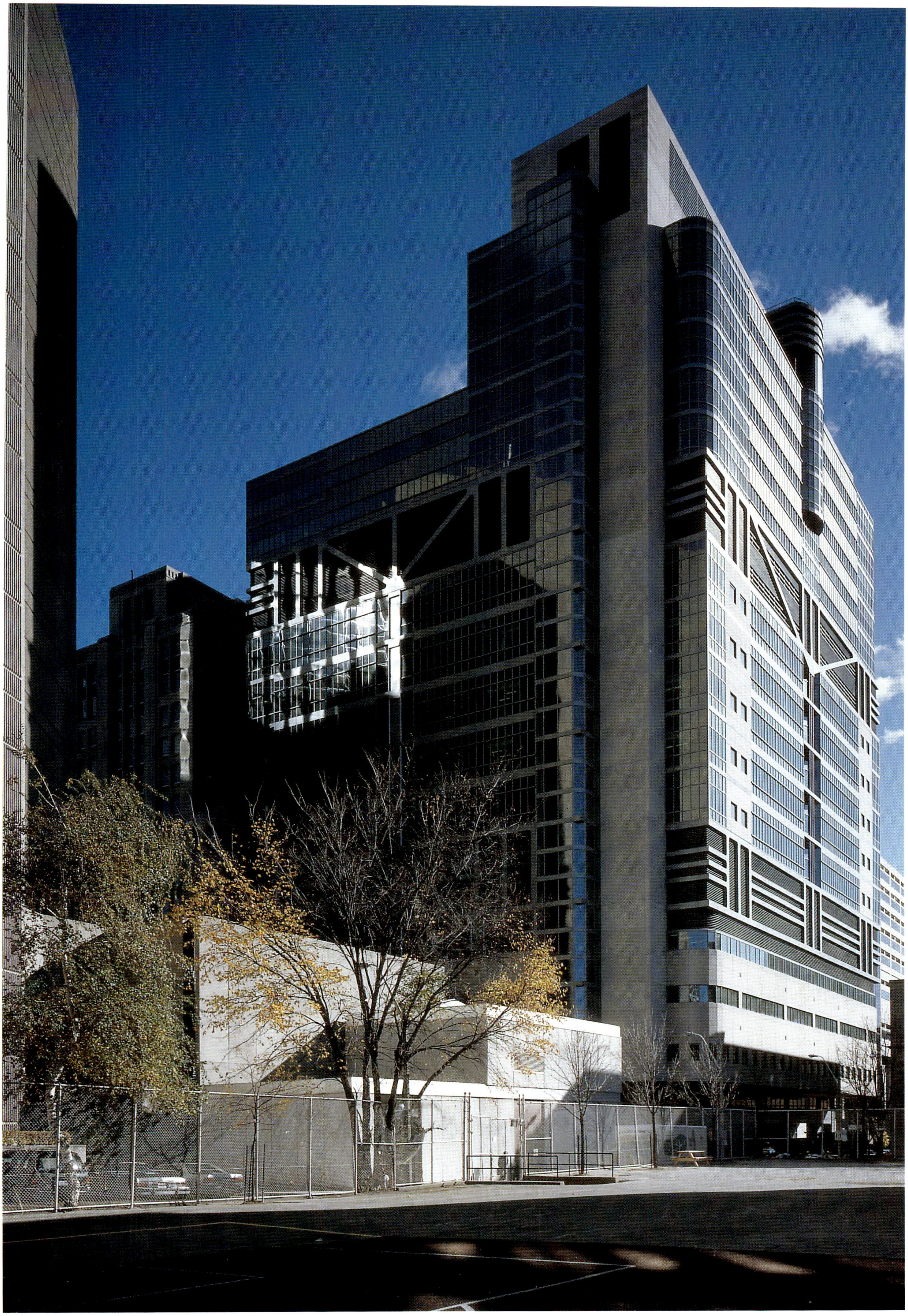

From bottom of page up, plans of the ground floor and the second floor.

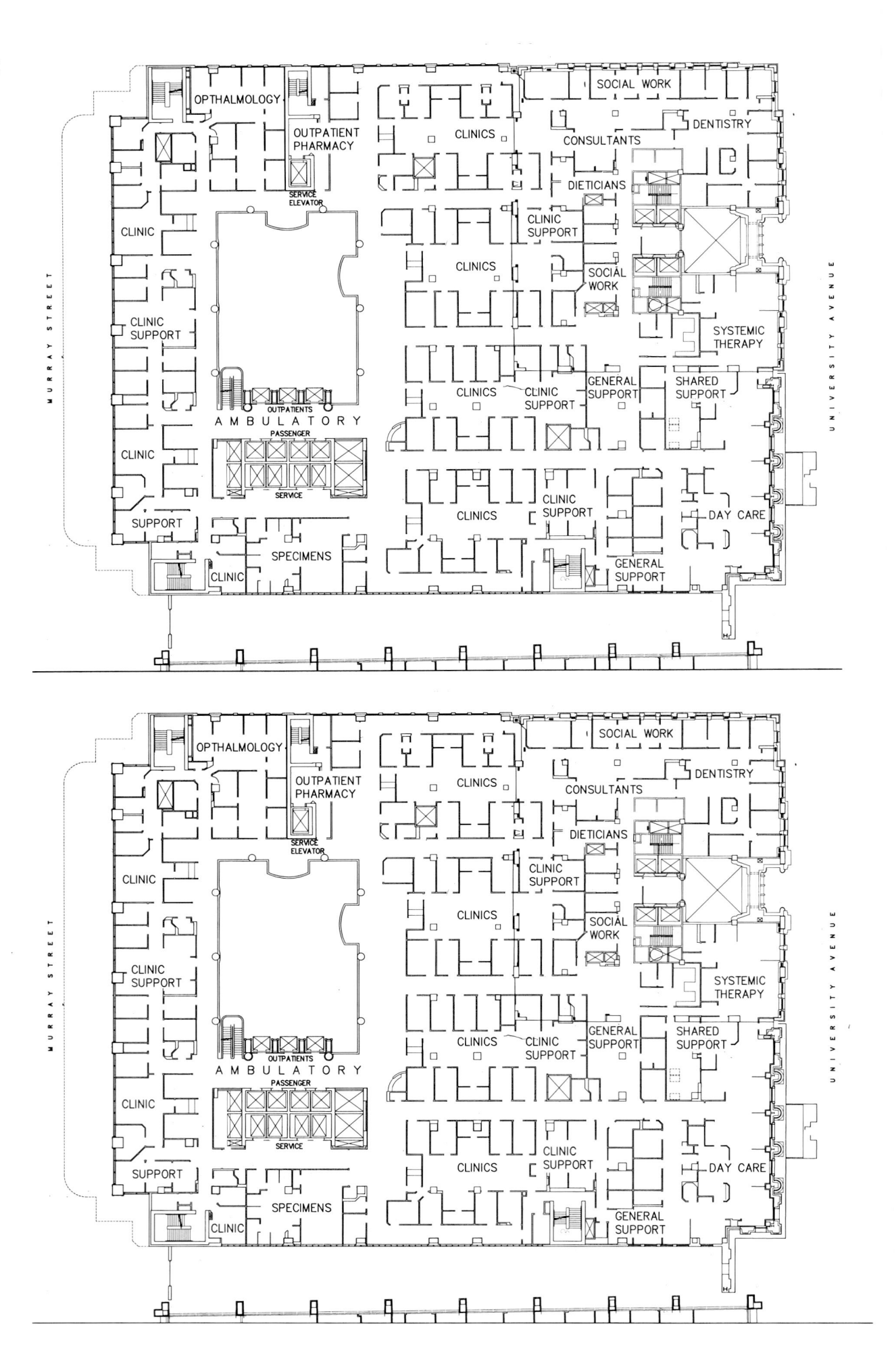

The research atrium, which sits between the outpatient atrium and the bedroom court. The hospital has been organized vertically around two atria and divided into four sectors stacked on top of each other.

Detail of the skylight at the top of the research atrium letting in natural light.

The outpatient atrium is landscaped and has a glass skylight with borrowed light from the research atrium.
Bottom of page, one of the teaching theatres for the university clinic.

95

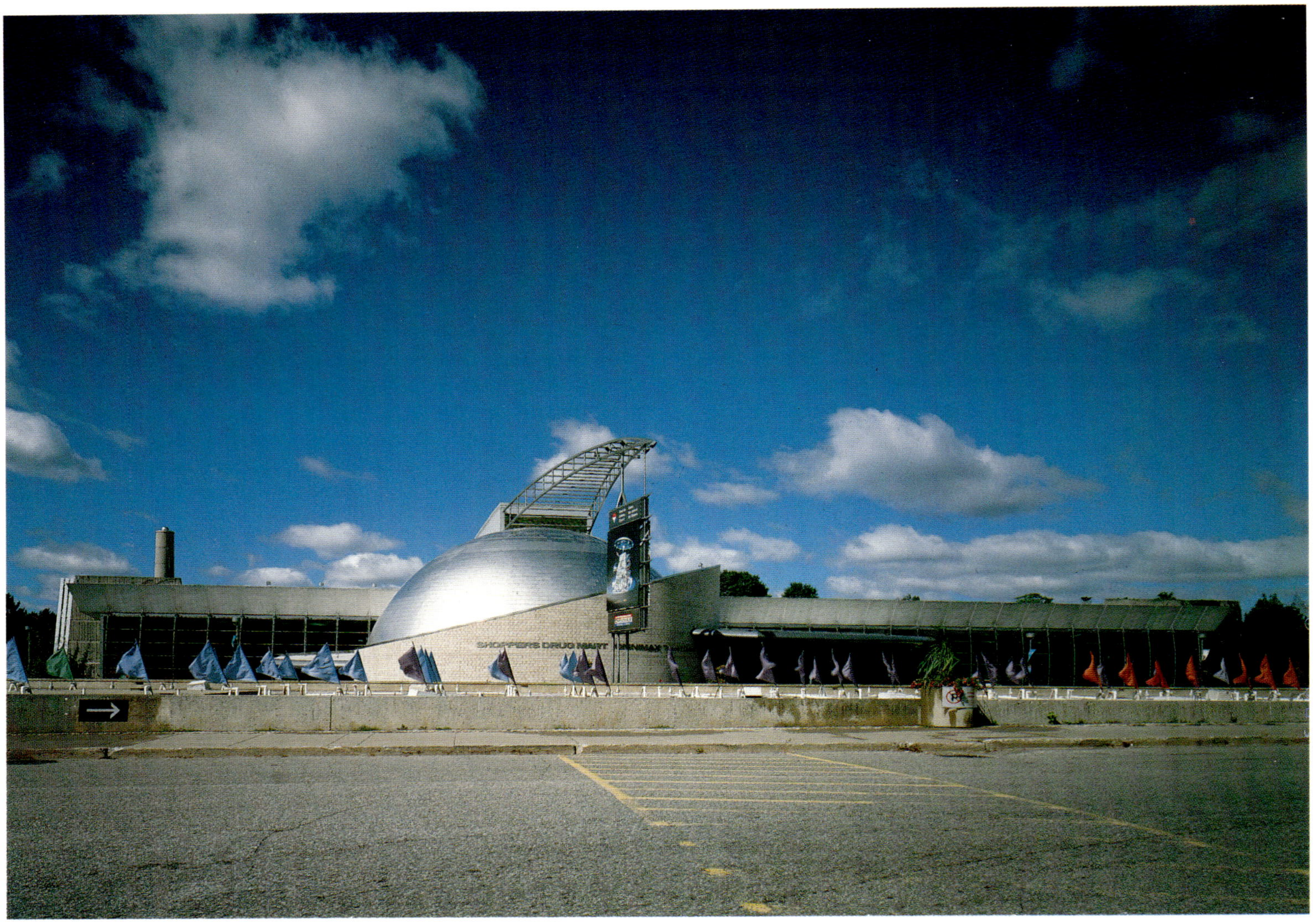

Ontario Science Centre - OMNIMAX® Cinema and Renovations

North York, Ontario

In order to revitalize the Ontario Science Centre, a major tourist attraction which opened in 1969, the firm redesigned the entrance pavilion of the Centre, which involved a total area of 138,920-square feet. The addition of a new OMNIMAX® theatre (28,676-square feet) created a dramatic focus, inviting people to explore the wonders of the Centre. The 320-seat cinema, presents images on a dome screen, totally filling the viewer's field of vision in all directions, and showing scientific events in a close-to-reality image. Located in front of the reception building so that it can operate as part of the Centre itself or independently, the cinema helped to revise and clarify the existing entrance. The reception building features a two-storey glass wall and renovated ticketing, retail, and support amenities, as well as new dining and banquet facilities.

The powerful roof structure of the existing Centre remained untouched, but the main pedestrian entrance was moved from the second floor to the ground floor, opening up the whole facade. A new two-storey glass pavilion exposes the Centre's activities to outsiders and beckons the public to come in and explore. The OMNIMAX® theatre breaks the length of this facade, while displaying its fascinating theatre function to the street, and allowing visitors to view the complex projection apparatus from the lobby.

These changes now allow one to walk on the same level from the parking lot to the front entrance through the northern plaza, set in the apex of the OMNIMAX® theatre and the existing building. The plaza contains areas for passenger drop-off and scientific displays, and leads to the lobby where tickets can be purchased for the Centre, the OMNIMAX,® theatre, or both. From here, one can proceed to any destination - into the theatre watching the film equipment being raised into working position as one passes, or to the escalator which leads to the upper lobbies and the entrance to the exhibition areas.

At the south of the building, school buses are able to unload in a plaza separate from the general public. The lobby arrangement at the south apex is a pleasant way to deal with the happy activities of children coming and going, and provides locker and washroom facilities and allows easy access to the general public areas.

By replacing the existing concrete wall along the front of the facade with an inviting glass wall, allows visitors to see directly into the second floor from the first floor lobby, and opens up the back wall of the science store so that it is visible from below. As well, the restaurant on the lower floor has been extended into this area, with an upper floor balcony providing views from above. Visitors to the Science Centre are able to take an escalator from the lower lobby up to the second floor. Those who have seen the OMNIMAX® movie can leave the theatre via the upper level bridges that lead onto the second floor and into the exhibition area.

Nothing in the architectural arrangement of this building is superfluous. Every element used has been chosen with care to achieve the Centre's goals and to reinforce the power of the present structure. Its commanding roof will remain, now floating over an elegantly designed glass wall opening the Centre to the public.

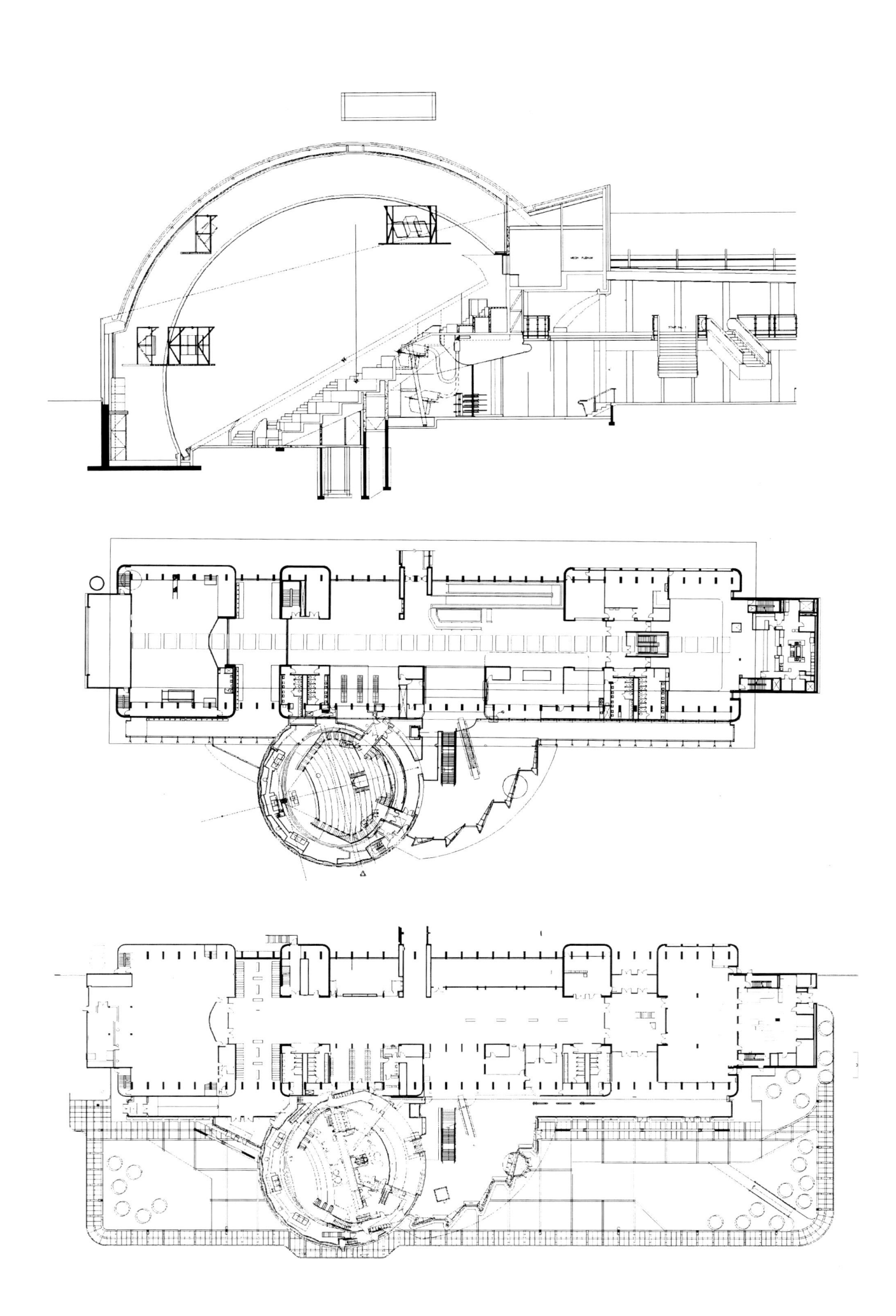

From bottom of page up, plans of the ground floor, second floor, and section through the Omnimax.

Aerial view and, bottom of page, the new all-glass entrance facade replacing the existing concrete wall.

Bottom, details of the school entrance showing the cylindrical structure housing the Omnimax movie theater. Top, general public entrance.

A detail of the new glass facade below the existing concrete roof allowing visitors to see directly into the two levels of the building from the outside.

The entrance to the Omnimax, with the new two-storey glass pavilion which opens the interior activities up to the outside and beckons the public to come in and explore.

Top, the lower lobby showing the reception around which the centre's activities unfold. Bottom, the view from the second floor into the lower lobby.

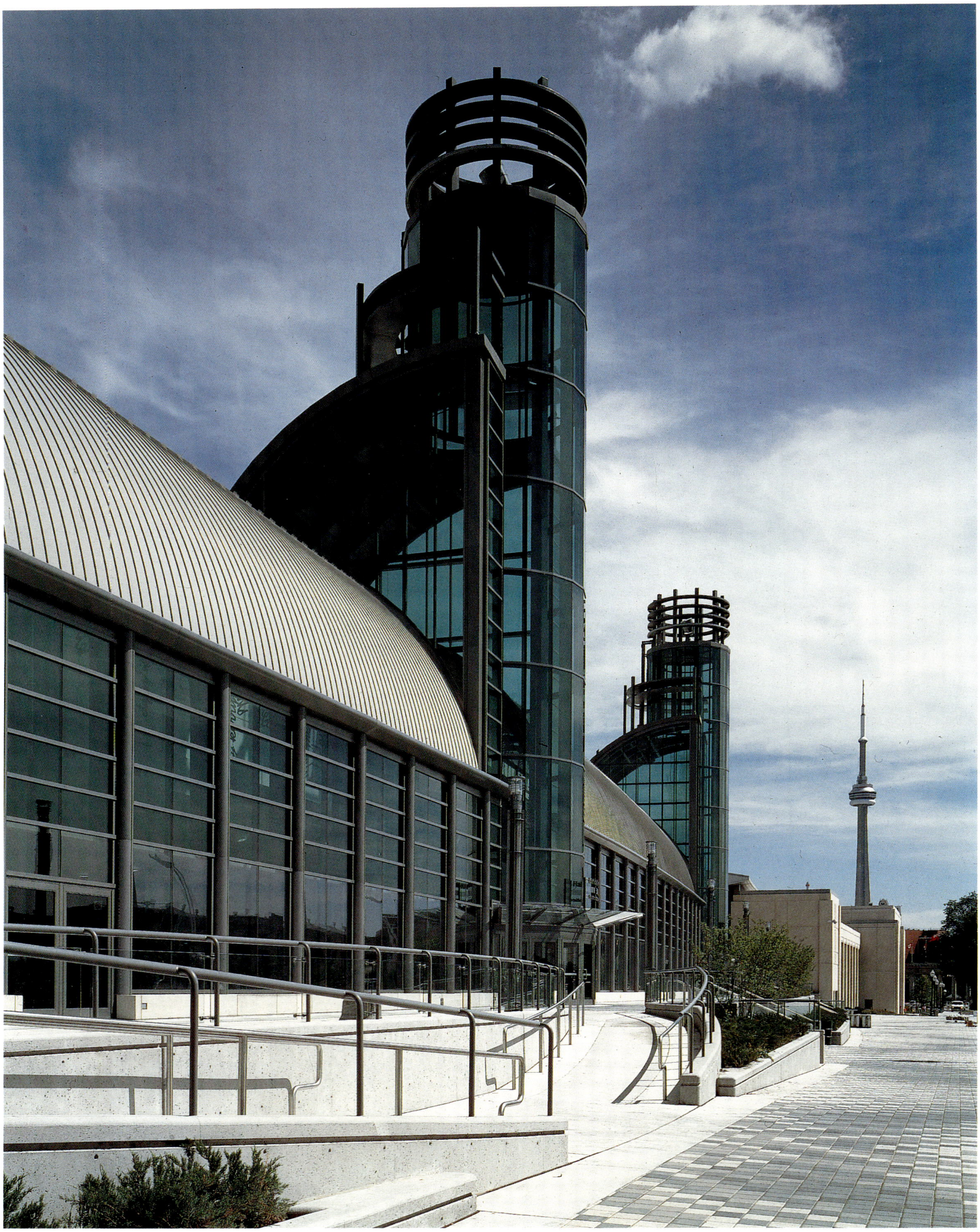

National Trade Centre at Exhibition Place
Toronto, Ontario

The design programme of the National Trade Centre required additional exhibition space equal to more than seven football fields. Such a building would result in a structure that would dominate Exhibition Place. The challenge was not only to provide the requisite space, but to make it function effortlessly, and to fold it seamlessly into the surrounding urban setting. The new exhibition facility, with the Coliseum and the Industrial Building to the north and the Automotive Building to the south, would provide more than 1,000,000-square feet of exhibition space.

The new Main Hall serves as the heart of the Centre and as its main exhibition space. It is divided into four separate rooms which can be used in conjunction with each other or separately, and can be changed into various configurations. To de-emphasize the Hall itself to let the exhibitors take centre stage, a buff monochromatic colour was used throughout. The floor of the Hall is organized on a 10 foot x 10 foot module and services such as electricity are provided from below the floor on the same modular basis. Columns are spaced at 90-feet and 120-feet intervals to achieve maximum flexibility of space. A slightly curved roof not only provides for an open and delightful space, but also reduced the construction cost.

There is a transition space between the Main Exhibition Hall and the Grand Concourse that contains meeting rooms, washrooms, registration areas, etc. The meeting rooms can be accessed from both the Concourse and the Exhibition Hall. They can be connected to the Main Hall as additional exhibition space or used independently from the Grand Concourse. A large kitchen services the Centre and is located at the west end.

A swing space has been built between the Main Exhibition Hall and the old Coliseum and Industrial Building and allows all three buildings to be used as one unit or separately, as required. The swing space is so named because it can be used in two different ways: it can serve as an addition to the Main Hall (as an exhibition area), or it can simply be used as an entrance foyer for the Coliseum and Industrial Buildings. The splendid historic facade of the Coliseum Building has been reconstructed and faces into the swing space which is covered over by a semi-circular skylight, giving the facade of the Coliseum plasticity and importance.

Along the south side of the Main Hall there is a 1,400-foot Grand Concourse separated from the Main Hall by a transition space. The Concourse, with its stunning lighted steel ribs, which curve from the rooftop to ground level, go step-by-step from one end of the continuous interior walkway to the other. This allows visitors to enter or bypass any portion of the exhibition spaces, as they desire.

By facing it in a mirror-like image, the east end of the Concourse reflects the form of the Automotive Building. It is used as a registration area and also serves as an entrance to the tunnel which connects the Automotive Building to the National Trade Centre. This allows the old building to be accessed effortlessly when additional exhibition space is required.

The Grand Concourse opens up visually to Princes Boulevard (to the south of the National Trade Centre), through a continuous, slightly curved, glass wall. The Concourse is at the same level as the Exhibition Hall, which was determined by the existing level of the Coliseum. This allows for a seamless interchange of Exhibition Hall-related traffic with Concourse traffic. Princes Boulevard, however, is 1.7-metres lower than the Concourse. An elegant arrangement of terraces, stairs and ramps on the exterior mitigate the difference in levels between the Concourse and the Boulevard by stepping down from one level to the other. These terraces can also be used for stands at the Indy races, which are held there.

The glass front of the Grand Concourse is punctuated by four 100-foot-high Tower Beacons, which visually reduce its length, and at the same time add a sense of celebration endemic to exhibition buildings.

These glass beacons enhance and strengthen the exterior facade and invite people to enter the building. At night, searchlights shoot light into the skies. The searchlights are installed at the apex of each tower and are used to visually announce events at the Centre as far as 20 miles away. These four high towers respond to Exhibition Place's existing 19th century tower pattern.

The composition integrates itself into the urban pattern of Exhibition Place. It responds to the Beaux Arts design of the Princes Gate and the Automotive Building to the east. Toward the west, its glass facade relates itself to Stanley Barrack Park and to views of the lake. The curve of the Concourse follows the curve of Princes Boulevard.

Site plan and ground-floor plan.

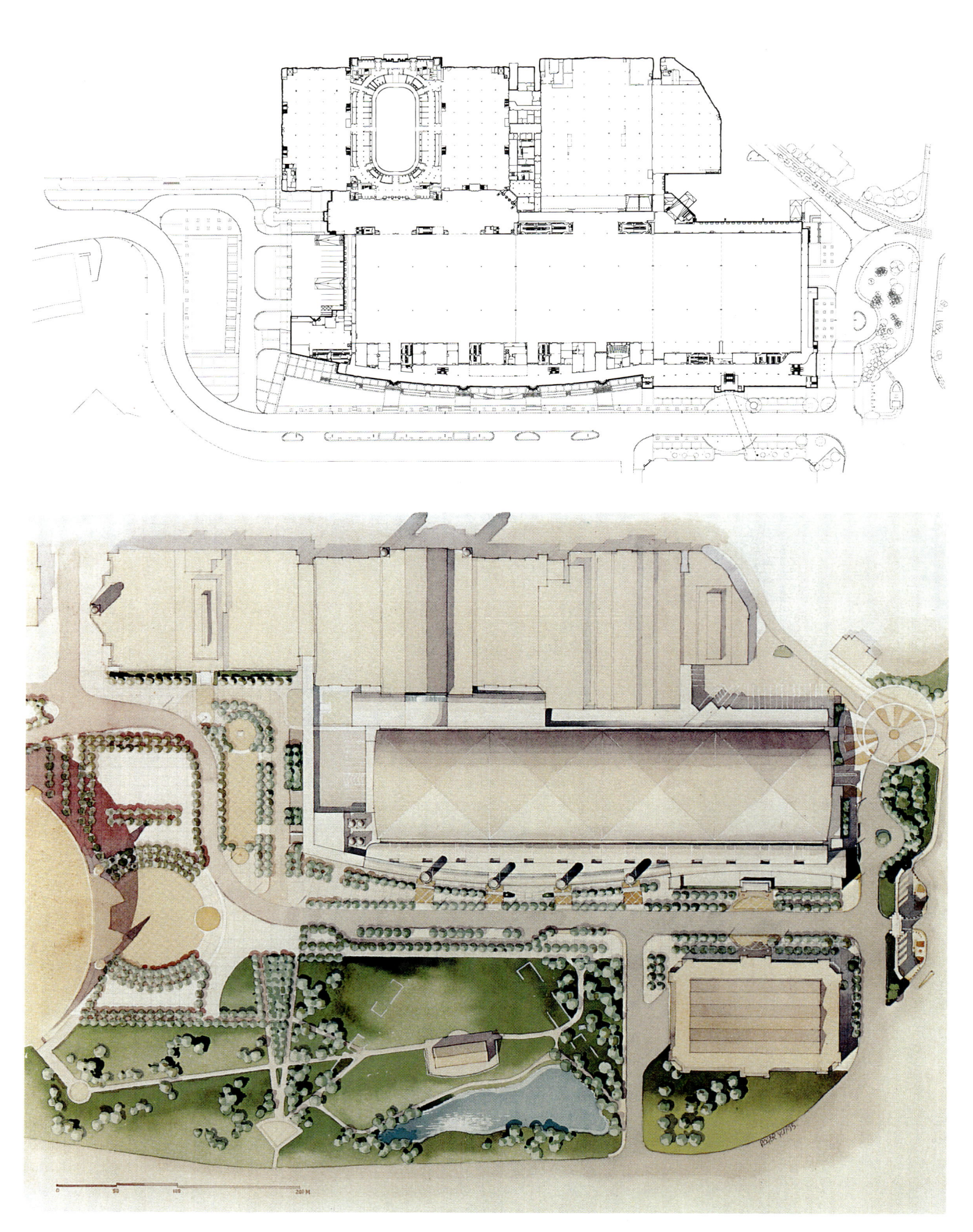

The glass front of the Grand Concourse, punctuated by four 100-feet-tall Tower Beacons that reduce its length visually and, at the same time, create that sense of celebration endemic to exhibition buildings.

Top, the east facade which opens onto the landscaped plaza, reflecting to the south the Automotive Building. Bottom, the entrance from the TTC station at the north.

Top, the glass towers enhance and strengthen the south facade and invite people to enter the building. Bottom, the east section of the south facade reflects the Automotive Building which sits across the boulevard. Well curved towers face the public park.

Bottom, details of the inside of one of the towers and of the corridor inside the glass facade and, top, the main concourse.

The exterior entrance into the swing space.

The inside of the Main Hall. The floor of the hall is constructed around a 10x10 foot module with columns spaced at 90 feet and 120 feet to create flexible exhibition space. Below, detail of the east corridor connecting the transit entrance on the east side to the main concourse.

One of the lecture rooms in the Transition Space which separates the Grand Concourse from the Main Hall.
Bottom, entrance from the parking evel into the Grand Concourse.

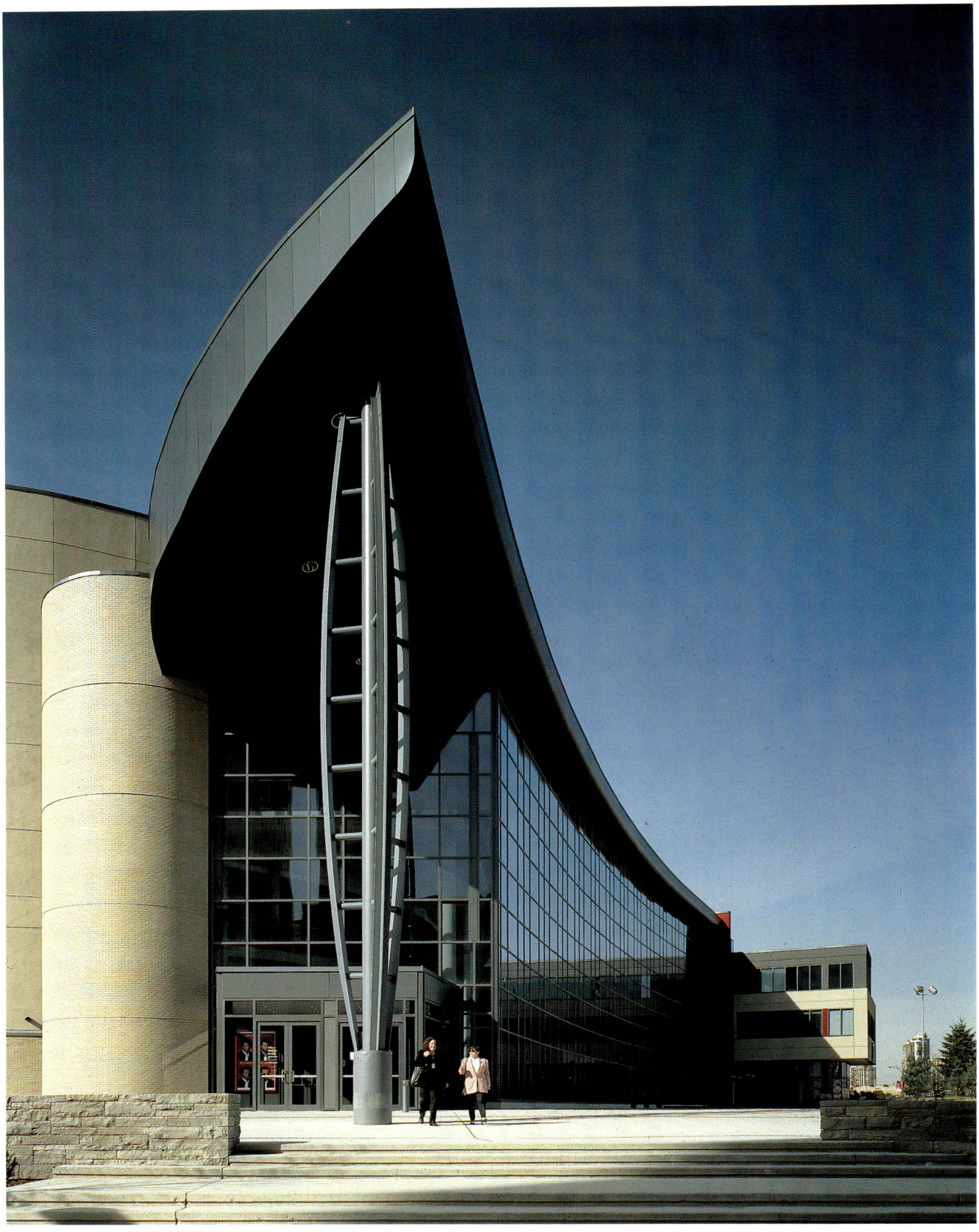

The Living Arts Centre
Mississauga, Ontario

Located on a six-acre site north of the city centre, this innovative 210,000-square foot facility is symbolic of a new era. It not only creates a symbiosis of the visual and performing arts, which have previously been separated, but also links them to newer branches which have evolved as a result of the use of computers and other tools of the communication age.

After many years of discussion with the community, the final programme for the Centre included the musical and the performing arts, but in a way in which community involvement and world-class performance would go hand-in-hand. This process resulted in the careful selection of the most important elements which would make this new concept possible, within a limited budget.

The main venue is the 1,300-seat Hammerson Hall, suitable for ballet, theatre, symphony or opera performances, and has a fully equipped stage house. The audience is arranged in a horseshoe form around the stage on three levels, so that no seat is further than 95-feet away from the stage.

A second venue for the performing arts is Theatre II, a recital hall which accommodates approximately 400 people and is to be used for theatrical and musical events. The classic shoe box shape, which provides excellent acoustics, has been used here. Movable seats on the ground floor and around the balcony in the mezzanine can be utilized to create a close relationship between the audience and the performer. A working grid spans the entire theatre. The removable seating allows various types of performances to be held (e.g., variations of experimental performances, dinner theatre, etc.).

In addition to these two main venues, there are several lecture halls and rehearsal spaces, including the 110-seat Theatre III. As well, there are music studios and practice cubicles which allow for the development of a rich music repertoire and all the necessary back-of-house facilities for the performing arts.

The visual arts studios (as well as some of the previously-mentioned facilities for music) are located in the three-storey Visual Arts Galleria which is linked to the performing arts component. Every effort was made to bring all the arts together in their daily routine, yet allow for the necessary segregation of the various activities during performance times. Windows into the various activity areas allow visitors to view the artists at work.

Studios which utilize heavy materials and equipment are located on the first level. Glass overhead doors open onto an adjacent park so that some activities can be performed in the open during the summer. At the northeast entrance a restaurant serves food throughout the day in an inexpensive yet elegant way. The restaurant can be used to create a delightful dinner atmosphere at performance time, and can then be changed back to its bar-like configuration after the performance. Across from the restaurant, the television control room for Cable 10 sits behind a glass screen. The remainder of the floor houses recreation rooms and assembly spaces for visiting groups and school children, as well as the necessary loading facilities for the entire complex. The second floor contains the previously mentioned music facilities, computer studios and a large two-story rehearsal hall, as well as centrally located, yet hidden mechanical spaces. The third floor contains a number of artists' studios for painting and sculpturing, which require overhead lighting, as well as a television studio for Cable 10.

One of the most important considerations in the Centre's design was to create a traffic network which would provide easy access both directly to and between the facilities, but would also produce exciting and pleasant places which would encourage social encounters, as the interchange of ideas is one of the most important aspects of a centre such as this.

The main purpose of this building is evident within the three-storey Atrium. It demonstrates that the arts are interactive events, created by people for people, not something outside of the community, but something very much a part of the community. The architectural treatment is, therefore, not one of a temple of culture, but of a workplace where one creates culture. It is a space that can withstand tough contact with vibrant activities, and yet still exude the joy of anticipation for the activities within. The juxtaposition of masonry and framing, concrete construction and steel construction all serve to create a joyful complexity.

From bottom of page up, plans of the ground floor, first floor and second floor.

Second Floor Legend

1. Concert Theatre - 2nd Balcony
2. Dance Studio
3. InfoStudy
4-5. Visiting Artists' Studio
6. Painting/Drawing
7. Printmaking/Fibre Arts
8. Artists' Lounge
9. Virtual Reality Studio
10. Discovery Deck
11. Community Broadcast
12. Public Elevators

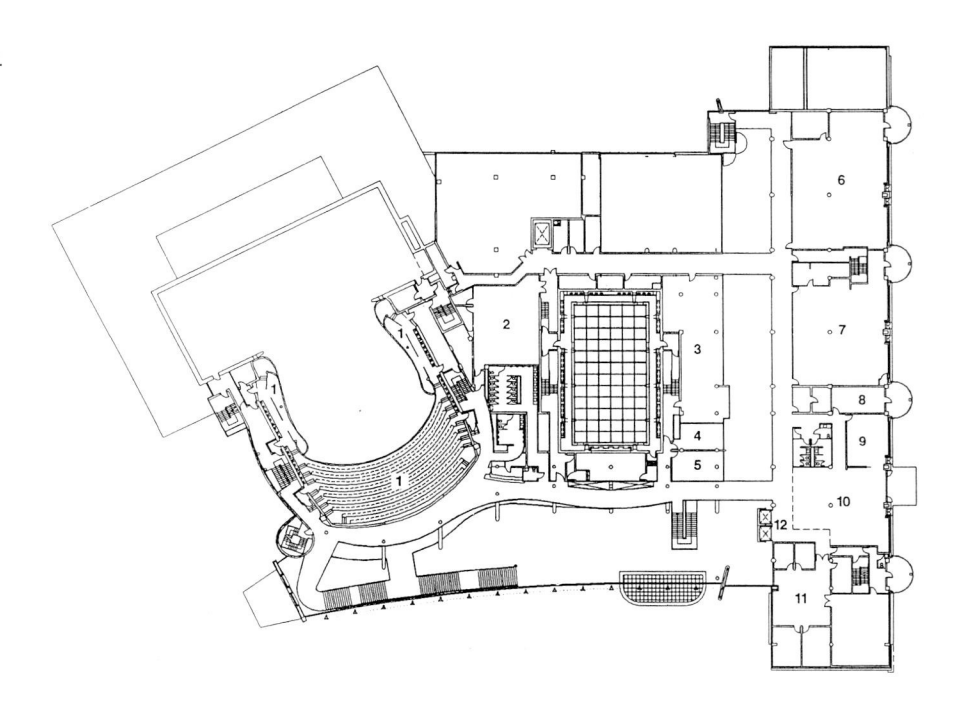

First Floor Legend

1. Concert Theatre - 1st Balcony
2. Theatre I - Mezzanine Levels I & II
3. Staging Room
4. Classroom I
5. Classroom II
6. Conference Room
7. Photography
8. Exhibition Display Space
9-10. Music Recording Studio
11-12. Music Studio
13. Volunteer room
14. Digital Arts Studio
15. Computer Teaching
16. Image Shop
17. Kidspace
18. Subscription/ Foundation Offices
19. Café
20. Public Elevators
21. Administration Offices
22. Central Communication

Ground floor Legend

1. Concert Theatre
2. Stage
3. Theatre II
4. Theatre III
5. Performance Hospitality
6. Ceramics/Pottery
7. Raku Kiln
8. Glass
9. Sculpture
10. Jewellery
11. Wood
12. Community Broadcast
13. Restaurant
14. Box Office
15. Gift Shop
16. Public Elevators
17. Atrium
18. Galleria
19. South Entrance
20. East Entrance
21. North Entrance
22. West Entrance
23. Stage Door

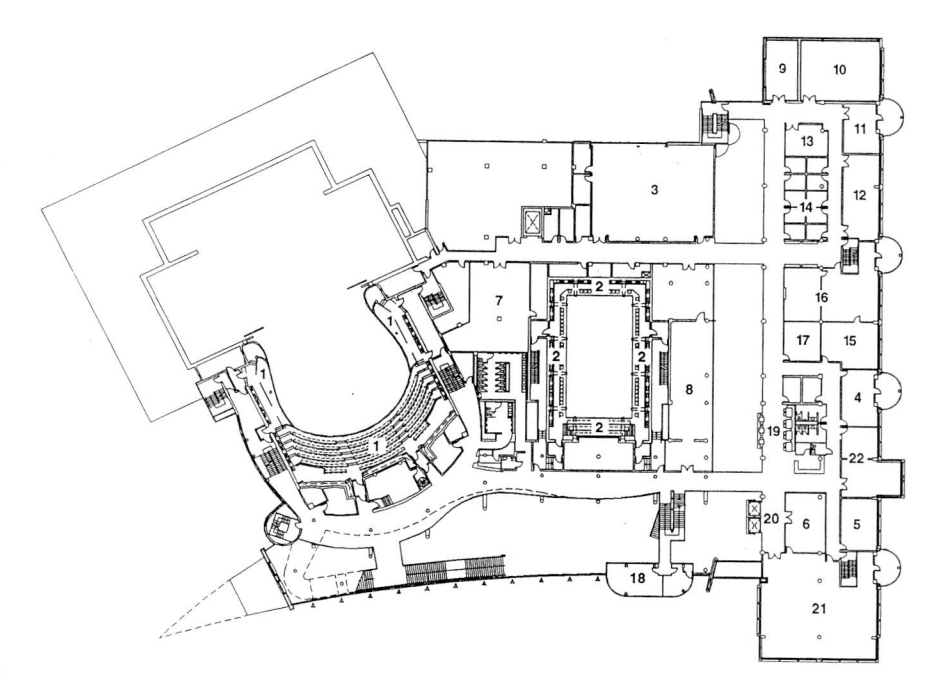

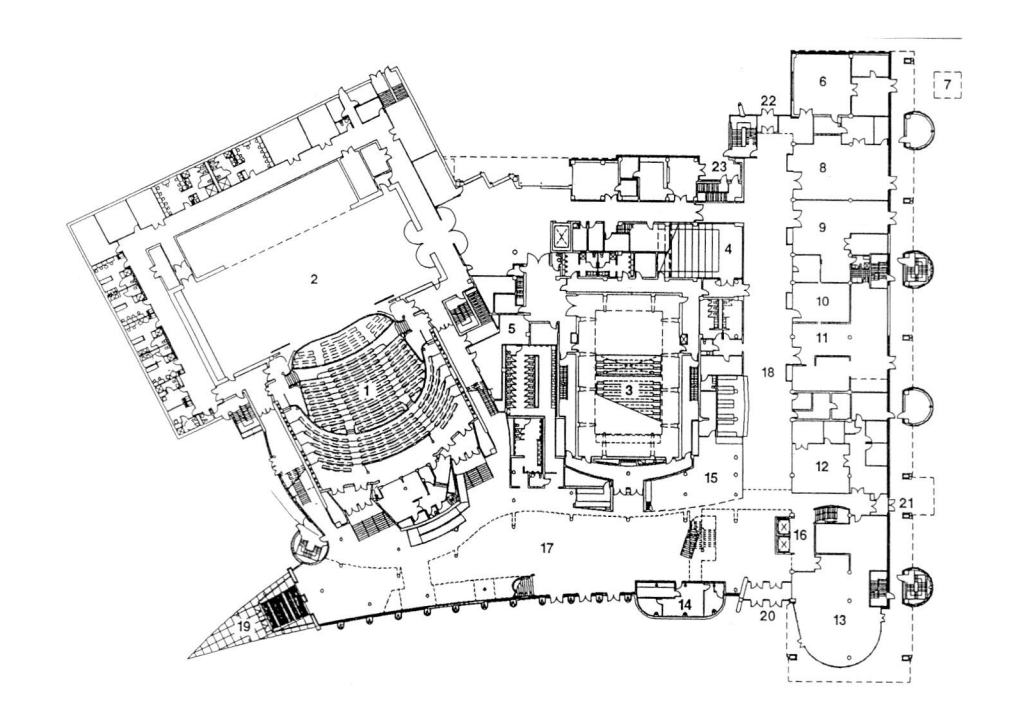

The all-glass main facade
leading into the atrium
with a view of city hall.

Right, view into Visual Art Gallery. Bottom, the atrium is defined by a carved 60-foot high glassed surface supported by a spider's web of trusses.

Top, view of the Visual Art Gallery from Atrium. Bottom, a view into the atrium from the Hammerson Hall upper level towards the junction with the Visual Art Gallery.

Recital hall for approximately 400 people to be used for theatrical and musical as well as community events.

120

Details of Hammerson Hall, which is arranged in a horseshoe-shape around the stage on three levels, so that no seat is more than 95 feet from the stage.

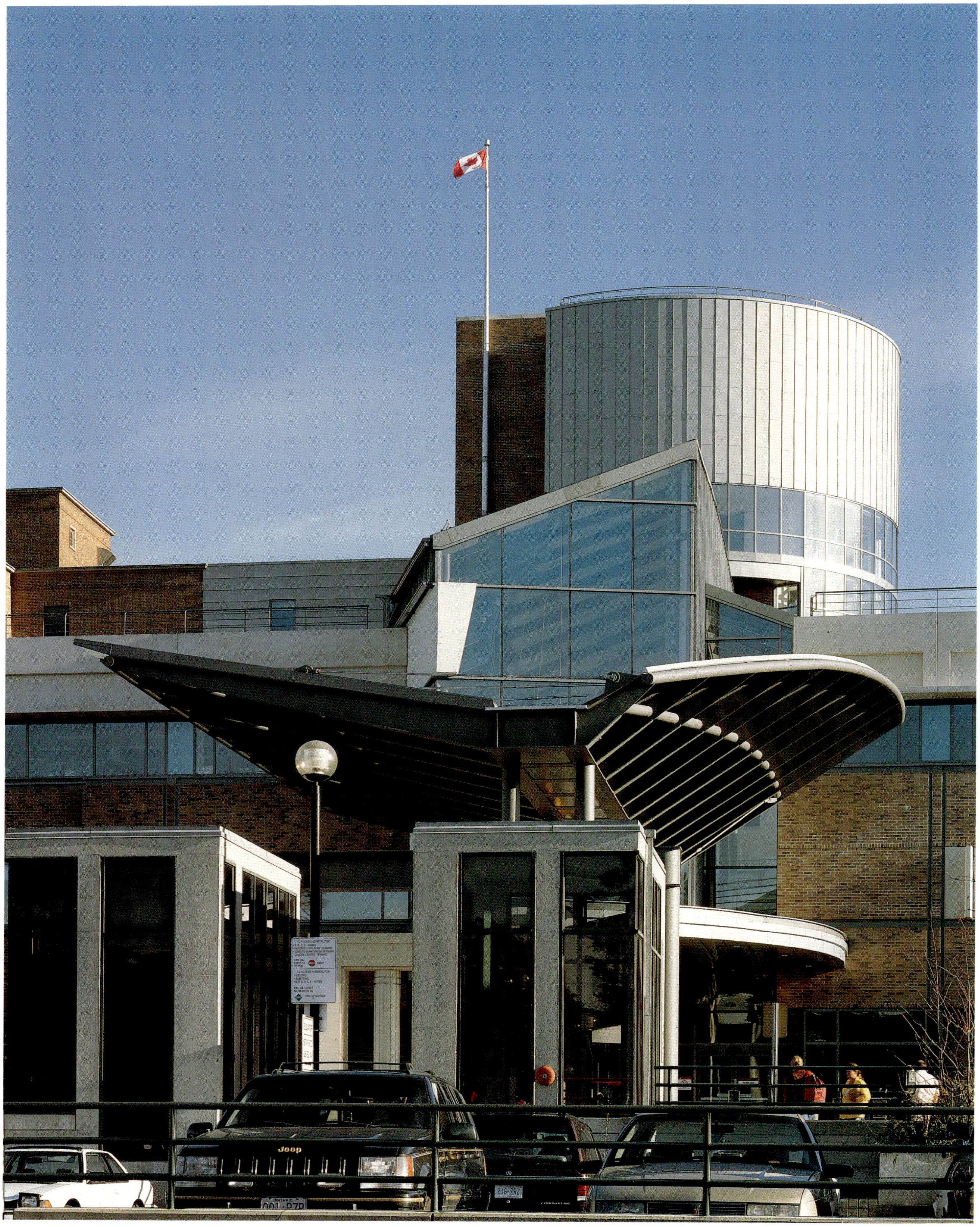

Sunnybrook Health Science Centre Clinical Services Wing

North York, Ontario

This 335,000-square foot addition, designed to blend with the existing University of Toronto's Sunnybrook Health Science Centre, represents Phase II of Zeidler Roberts Partnership's Master Plan for this 1,000-bed tertiary care teaching facility. The facilities in the new Clinical Services Wing are strategically located to ensure important adjacencies to existing or expanding facilities remaining in the existing building, as well as link the Health Science Centre with the complex's parking garage. Connections are made by means of tunnels, bridges and a nine-storey elevator tower which complements the Centre's clock tower. The Wing's design also facilitates future vertical expansion.

The Wing is located at the inner angle of the long and L-shaped Centre to bring these services close to the centre of the hospital. At the same time, the new Clinical Services Wing includes the Centre's new main entrance which features a large retail space (including pharmacy, medical retail service, gift shop and cafeteria) as an amenity and profit centre. The Entrance Canopy, the Galleria and the Atrium are conceived as a series of events that emphasize this entrance function.

The Entrance Canopy was created to herald the major drive-in entrance into the hospital, and at the same time to connect the parking garage stairs with the main entrance. A height had to be created to make it possible to have trucks drive under the canopy. The level below is the ambulance-patient entrance. The canopy was designed to create a visual connection with the Galleria.

The Galleria roof was formed to allow daylight to enter this space with minimal sun penetration and to give this space a feeling of movement. The lower Patient Entrance and the upper General Entrance were visually connected through an opening with glass stairs and a waterfall.

The Atrium is off the end of this entrance sequence and visually concludes this series of elements, yet at the same time allows views from the glass elevators into this space. The elevators distribute the general visitor traffic to the various floors. The Atrium space itself is created by two walls of the existing building, the central glass elevator core and the new wing, with the Intensive Care Unit waiting area facing this space. The roof is supported by six steel columns which branch out like trees at the top and each opens a skylight that sheds daylight into the space.

On the whole, the new facilities include: 16-bed O.R. Surgical Suite, 26-bed Induction/Post-Anaesthesia Care Unit, 18-bed CCU, 12-bed Cardiovascular ICU, expanded outpatient services (including Otolaryngology, Ophthalmology, Rheumatology, Dermatology, Orthopaedics, and Internal Medicine), expanded Radiology services, new Surgical Day Procedures services (incorporating specimen collection, testing centre, day surgery minor procedures, Urology/Cystoscopy, and Pain Clinic), Department of Anaesthesia, Ambulatory Care Centre, and Central Sterile Processing Department linked to the Surgical Suite. The Clinical Services Wing also provides a major source of support for the Centre's cancer services.

Details of the new wing of the Sunnybrook Health Sciences Centre. The building is located at the inner angle of the long, L-shaped centre to bring the new services closer to the centre of the hospital.

The main entrance to the new wing.

The atrium, created by two walls of the existing building, the central glass elevator core and the new wing, serves as the cafeteria for the whole hospital complex. The roof is supported by six steel columns, which branch out like trees, each opening into a skylight to bring daylight into the space.

Top, the view from elevation of public entrance gallery into the portal complex. Bottom, connection of ambulatory patient entrance with the public entrance gallery.

A view of the existing building walls forming two sides of the atrium.

The view of public entrance gallery towards elevator core with bridges connecting the new wing to the gallery.

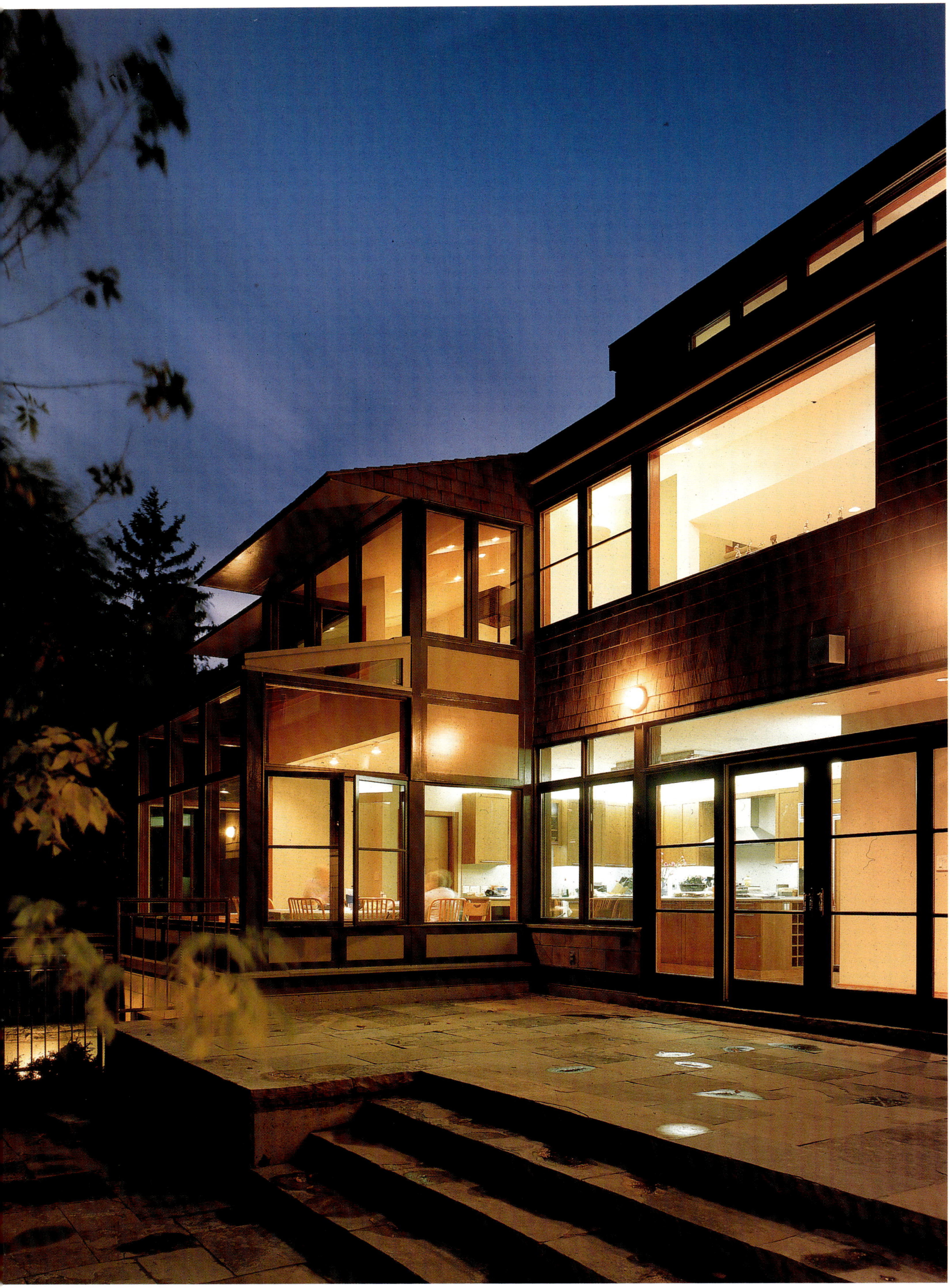

431 Glencairn Avenue
Toronto, Ontario

This new 7,500-square-foot residence is situated on a half-acre double lot and includes an attached 11,000-square-foot interior swimming pool area, which is accessible from the house. Designed for a family with young children, this two-storey structure has lofts over the children's bedrooms and a full lower level. Features include a double height living room, seven bedrooms, including a master bedroom suite, a large eat-in kitchen and a two-car garage. The layout allows for the separation of formal events from informal activities, with the main entrance leading to the formal spaces and a separate entrance for day-to-day activities. Two generous studio spaces provide a comfortable setting for the owners to work at home. Custom finishes such as cherry wood cabinets, casework and doors, steel railings, and colourful gilt-like patterns of ceramic tile, provide visually interesting details throughout the interior. Plenty allows for a future elevator, should one ever be required. This modern style brick and wood shingle residence is set back 60-feet from the street to relate to the existing street from the adjacent houses. The massing has also been carefully adjusted to keep it in scale with the surrounding older houses. In the front, a well landscaped area with the birch trees creates a forecourt which screens the house. The south-facing garden facade is mostly glass, with the principle rooms of the house opening onto patio areas. These connect with the terrace of the pool, which is enclosed by large sliding-glass doors. In the summer, two walls of the pool can slide open towards the garden to provide an outdoor setting for entertainment and leisure activities.

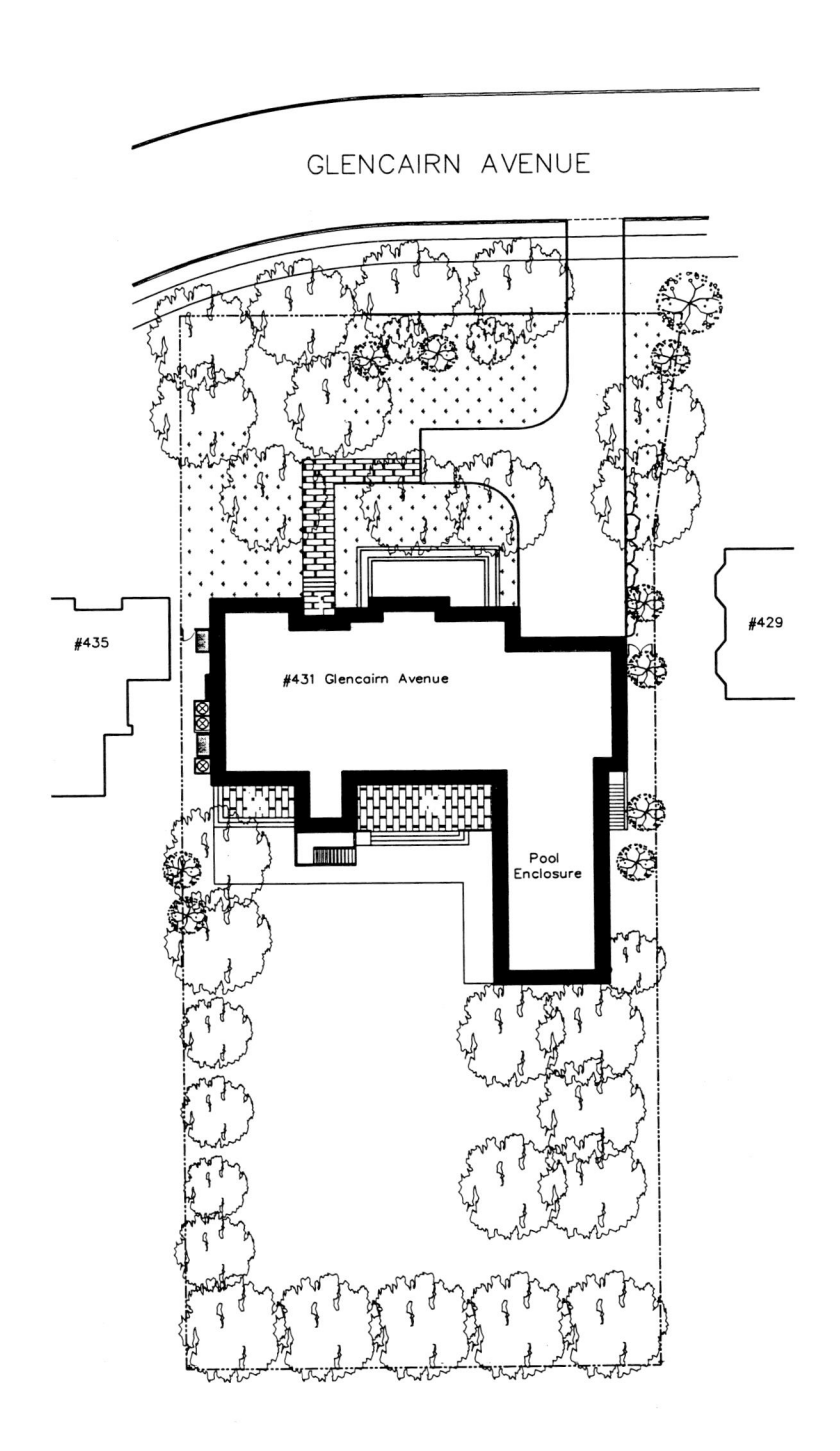

From bottom up, ground-floor plan, plans of the loft and second floor plan.

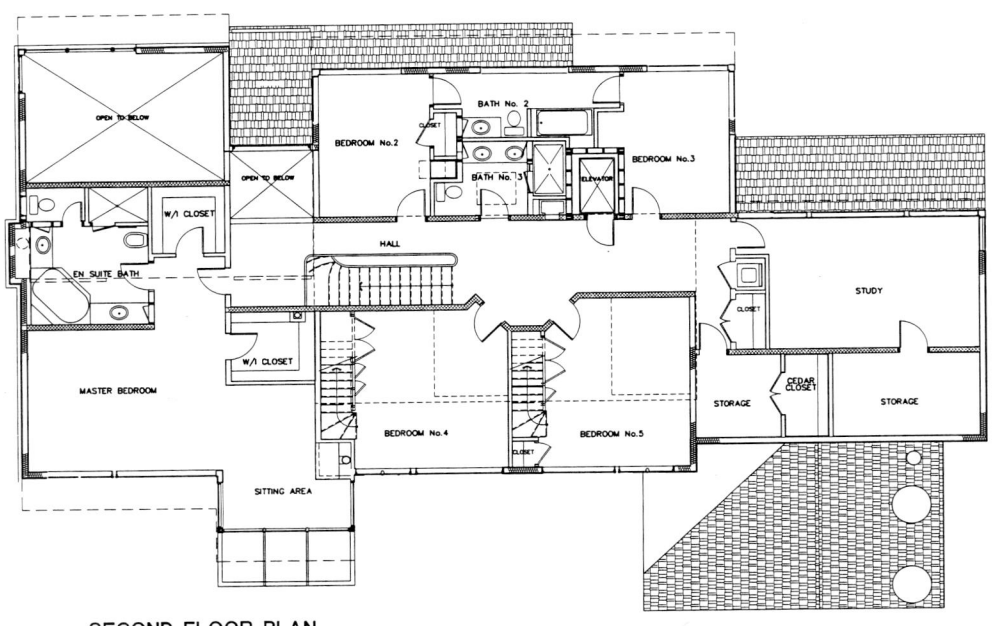

SECOND FLOOR PLAN

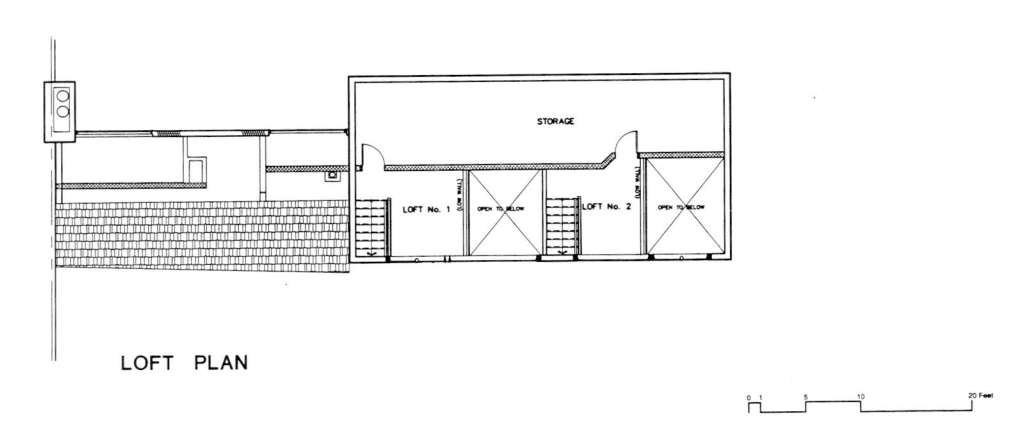

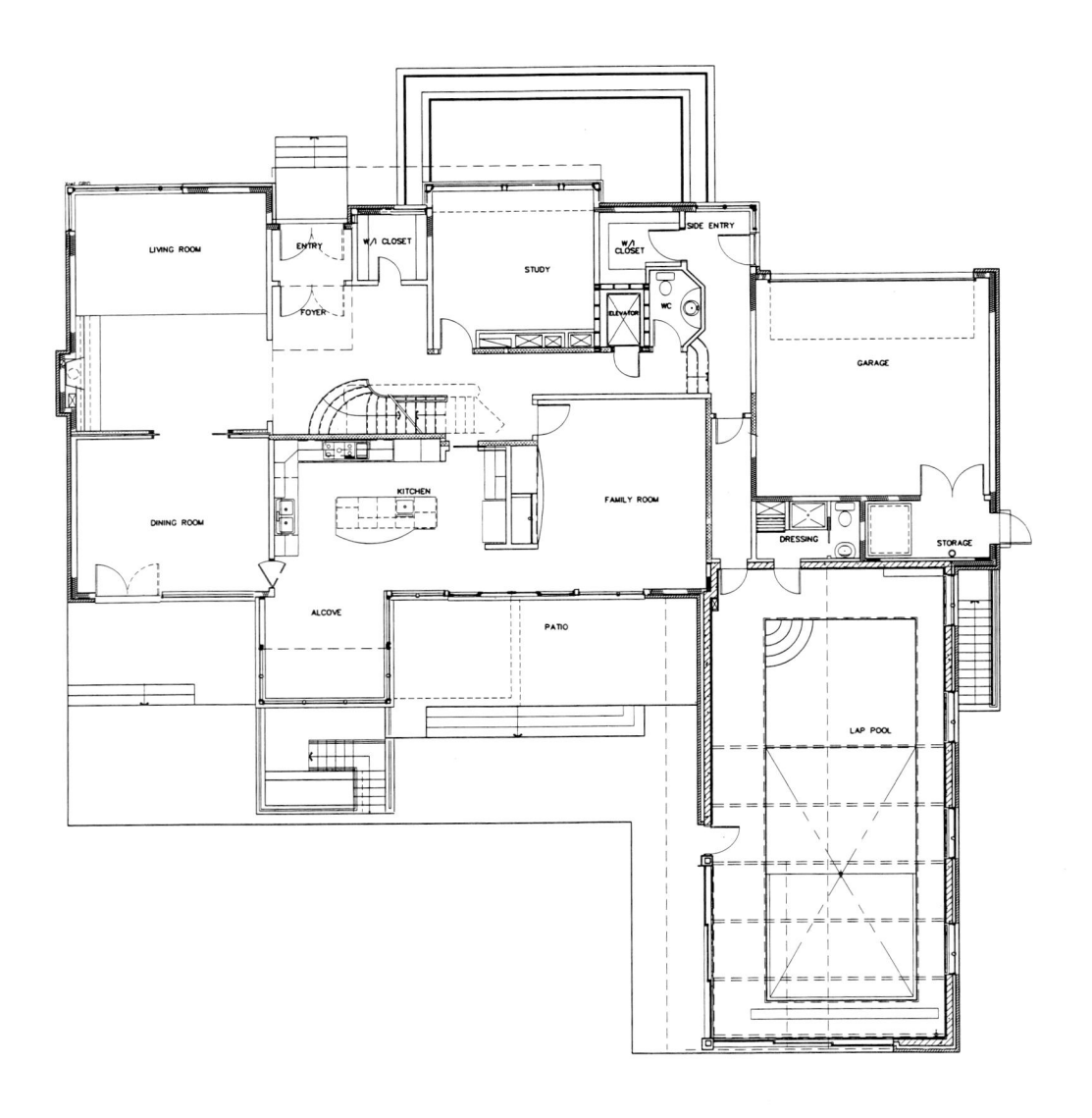

LOFT PLAN

Garden court of the residence, showing windows of the loft space.

Top, the Solarium showing the eating nook in the kitchen. Bottom of page, details of the interior finishings.
Opposite page, the dining room and kitchen seen from the swimming pool.

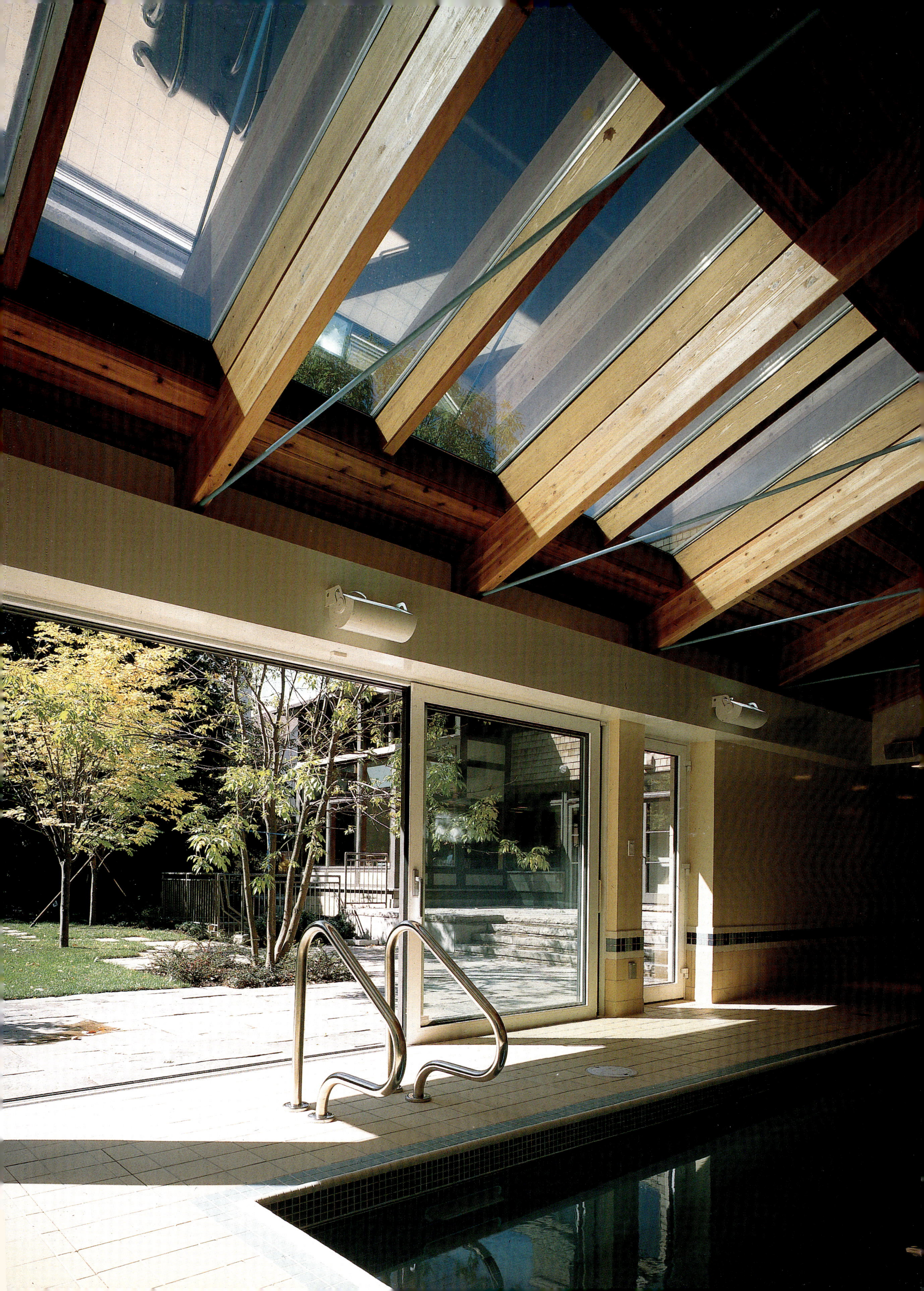

List of works

Seoul Canadian Embassy, Seoul, Korea, 1997.
A. Grenville and William Davis Courthouse, Brampton, Ontario, 1997.
Humber River Regional Hospital (Additions and Renovations), North York, Ontario, 1997.
Hong Kong Canadian International Hospital & Technical Exchange Centre, Hong Kong, 1996.
Exton Square Mall (Renovations and Additions), Exton, Pennsylvania, 1995.
Institute for Applied Health Science. Mohawk College and McMaster University, Hamilton, Ontario, 1995.
431 Glencairn, Toronto, Ontario, 1995/1997.
National Trade Centre at Exhibition Place, Toronto, Ontario, 1995/1997.
Hillsborough Court at Pacific Place, Scarborough, Ontario, 1994/1997
Ontario Science Centre. OMNIMAX® Cinema and Renovations, North York, Ontario, 1994/1996.
260 Russell Hill Road Condominium Design, Toronto, Ontario, 1994.
Embankment Place at Moscow International Business Centre, Moscow, Russia, 1994.
Nevis Four Seasons Resort. Phase II, 1994/1995.
York Woods Library Theatre (Additions And Renovations), North York, Ontario, 1993/1995.
Shanghai Xuhui International Tennis Club, Shanghai, China, 1993.
Herzzentrum (Heart Centre) Sachsen-Anhalt, Coswig, Germany, 1993.
Long-Term Care Facility, Dresden, Germany, 1993.
Dong Xiao Plaza, Guangzhou, China, 1993.
University of Toronto. Joseph L. Rotman Centre for Management, Toronto, Ontario, 1992/1995.
University of Toronto. Innis College Residence, Toronto, Ontario, 1992/1994.
University of Toronto. Parking Garage, Toronto, Ontario, 1992/1993.
The Living Arts Centre in Mississauga, Mississauga, Ontario, 1992/1997.
Beijing Capital International Airport. Terminal Concept Design, Beiing, China, 1992/1993.
Mühlendorf Housing Development, Teltow, Germany, 1992.
Suhl Civic Centre, Suhl, Germany, 1991/1995.
Columbus Centre of Marine Research and Exploration, Baltimore, Maryland, 1991/1995.
University of Maryland Medical System. The Homer Gudelsky Building, Baltimore, Maryland, 1991/1994.
BNI City, Wismar 46 Office Tower, Jakarta, Indonesia, 1990/1996.
CIBC DC/Menkes Development, Scarborough, Ontario, 1990.
Knightsbridge Green (formerly Portcullis), London, England, 1990.
Franklin Park (Renovations and Additions), Toledo, Ohio, 1990/1993.
CIBC Commerce Court Renewal, Toronto, Ontario, 1989/1994.
Cinedom in MediaPark, Cologne, Germany, 1989/1991.
Moscow Business Centre, Moscow, Russia, 1989.
Pacific Place Master Plan, Scarborough, Ontario, 1989/1990.
Ford Centre for the Performing Arts, North York, Ontario, 1989/1993.
Port East, London, England, 1988.
Port Vell, Barcelona, Spain, 1988.
Royal Palm Condominium Design, Richmond Hill, Ontario, 1988.
Eaton Tower/250 Yonge Street, Toronto, Ontario, 1988/1991.
Southtown. Marathon Railway Lands, Toronto, Ontario, 1984/1991.

Canadian Red Cross Society National Office, Ottawa, Ontario, 1983/1987.
Ontario Cancer Institute/Princess Margaret Hospital, Toronto, Ontario, 1987/1995.
Park Plaza Hotel (Renovations), Toronto, Ontario, 1987/1990.
Sherway Gardens. Phase IV, Etobicoke, Ontario, 1987/1989.
Confederation Life Canadian Head Office, Toronto, Ontario, 1987/1992.
MediaPark, Cologne, Germany, 1987/1992.
Fairview Mall (Renovations and Additions), North York, Toronto, Ontario, 1986/1988.
Central Guaranty Trust Computer Centre, Toronto, Ontario, 1986/1988.
Liberty Place. Phase II, Philadelphia, Pennsylvania, 1986/1990.
Metropolitan Toronto Archives and Records Centre, Toronto, Ontario, 1986/1991.
Royal York Hotel (Renovations and Addition), Toronto, Ontario, 1986/1991.
Pacific Centre (Renovations and Additions), Vancouver, British Columbia, 1985/1990.
Place Montréal Trust, Montréal, Québec, 1985/1989.
Raymond F. Kravis Centre for the Performing Arts, West Palm Beach, Florida, 1985/1992.
Ajax and Pickering General Hospital (Renovations), Ajax, Ontario, 1984/1994.
Davis Cabin, Georgian Bay, Ontario, 1983/1984.
Discovery Bay Golf Hotel Design, Hong Kong, 1983.
The Hospital for Sick Children. The Atrium (New Patient Tower), Toronto, Ontario, 1983/1993.
The Toronto Marriott Eaton Centre Hotel, Toronto, Ontario, 1983/1991.
Canada Place, Vancouver, British Columbia, 1982/1986.
The Mall (Metroplex Plaza), Kuala Lumpur, Malaysia, 1982/1986.
Ontario Pavilion. Expo '86, Vancouver, British Columbia, 1982/1986.
Pan Pacific Hotel, Vancouver, British Columbia, 1982/1986.
St. Paul's Hospital (Grey Nuns'), Saskatoon, Saskatchewan, 1982/1989.
Sunnybrook Health Science Centre/University of Toronto. Clinical Services Wing, North York, Ontario, 1982/1997.
Toronto World Trade Centre, Toronto, Ontario, 1982.
The Residences of the World Trade Centre, Toronto, Ontario, 1982/1990.
425 Bloor Street East, Toronto, Ontario, 1981/1987.
The College of Physicians & Surgeons of Ontario, Toronto, Ontario, 1981/1983.
The Gallery at Harborplace, Baltimore, Maryland, 1981/1987.
Mariner's Haven, Collingwood, Ontario, 1981/1990.
315 Queen Street West. Zeidler Roberts Partnership/Architects office, Toronto, Ontario, 1981/1983.
Stouffer Harborplace Hotel, Baltimore, Maryland, 1981/1988.
Stratford General Hospital (Additions), Stratford, Ontario, 1981/1991.
154 University Avenue. Union Bank of Switzerland (Canada), Toronto, Ontario, 1981/1989.
The Palisades Condominiums, Toronto, Ontario, Yerba Buena Gardens. Master Plan, San Francisco, California, 1980.
Agnes Macphail Public School, Milliken, Ontario, 1979/1981.
Brantford General Hospital (Renovations and Additions), Brantford, Ontario, 1979/1981.
33 Jackes Avenue, Toronto, Ontario, 1979/1988.
Queen's Quay Terminal, Toronto, Ontario, 1979/1983.
Fanshawe College. Master Plan, London, Ontario, 1978.
Ottawa Civic Hospital. Various Projects, Ottawa, Ontario, 1978/1984.
Rosedale Glen, Toronto, Ontario, 1978/1982.
Pickering Central Area Plan, Pickering, Ontario, 1977.

Rosenberg Residence, Kleinburg, Ontario, 1977/1980.
Shahara Resort Community. Master Plan, Alexandria, Egypt, 1977.
St. James Park, Toronto, Ontario, 1977.
Theme Park, Milton, Ontario, 1977.
The Mississauga Hospital (Renovations and Additions), Mississauga, Ontario, 1976/1983.
Young People's Theatre, Toronto, Ontario, 1976/1977.
207-219 Jarvis Street Historical Houses, Toronto, Ontario, 1976/1978.
Sussex Health Centre, Sussex, New Brunswick, 1975/1977.
Walter C. Mackenzie Health Sciences Centre, Edmonton, Alberta, 1975/1986.
Century Place, Belleville, Ontario, 1974/1976.
St. Lawrence Housing Project, Toronto, Ontario, 1974/1976.
Woodroffe Suburban Community, Ottawa, Ontario, 1974.
Mont Ste.-Marie, Lac Ste.-Marie, Quebec, 1973/1977.
Nanisivik Town Centre, Nanisivik, Northwest Territories, 1973/1977.
Sayers Residence, Terra Cotta, Ontario, 1973/1979.
Detroit Receiving Hospital and Wayne State University Health Care Institute, Detroit, Michigan, 1972/1979.
Dr. Everett Chalmers Hospital, Fredericton, New Brunswick, 1971/1976.
Dr. Georges L. Dumont Hospital, Moncton, New Brunswick, 1971/1975.
Saint John Regional Hospital, Saint John, New Brunswick, 1971/1982.
98 Queen Street East. Zeidler Roberts Partnership/Architects office, Toronto, Ontario, 1970/1971.
Vienna South Competition, Vienna, Austria, 1970.
University of Waterloo. Chemistry Building, Waterloo, Ontario, 1969/1971.
Cadillac Fairview Tower, Toronto, Ontario, 1969/1981.
Fanshawe College. Phase I, London, Ontario, 1969/1972.
Harbour City, Toronto, Ontario, 1969.
Number One Dundas Street West, Toronto, Ontario, 1969/1976.
Toronto Eaton Centre, Toronto, Ontario, 1969/1979.
Beaumont House, Toronto, Ontario, 1968/1969.
Ontario Place, Toronto, Ontario, 1968/1971.
Elliot Lake Secondary School, Elliot Lake, Ontario, 1967/1968.
McMaster University Health Sciences Centre, Hamilton, Ontario, 1967/1973.
Peterborough Police Building, Peterborough, Ontario, 1967/1971.
Ross Memorial Hospital (Renovations and Addition), Lindsay, Ontario, 1967/1970.
Korah Collegiate and Vocational School, Sault Ste.-Marie, Ontario, 1965/1968.
Madawaska Valley District High School, Barry's Bay, Ontario, 1965/1968.
Osler School of Nursing, North York, Ontario, 1965/1970.
Thomas A. Stewart High School, Peterborough, Ontario, 1965/1968.
University of Guelph. Physical Sciences Complex, Guelph, Ontario, 1965/1969.
Ajax Municipal Centre, Ajax, Ontario, 1965/1967.
Guelph General Hospital (Addition and Renovations), Guelph, Ontario, 1965/1968.
Ajax Centennial Memorial Arena, Ajax, Ontario, 1964/1965.
Scarborough Centennial Recreation Centre, Scarborough, Ontario, 1964/1967.
Whitby General Hospital, Whitby, Ontario, 1964/1970.
Grandview Avenue Public School, Oshawa, Ontario, 1964/1965.
Grant Sine Public School, Cobourg, Ontario, 1964/1965.
Peterborough Centennial Museum, Peterborough, Ontario, 1964/1965.
Pickering Municipal Building, Pickering, Ontario, 1964/1967.
Campbellford Memorial Hospital, Campbellford, Ontario, 1963/1964.
Crestwood Secondary School, Peterborough, Ontario, 1963/1964.
Douglas Memorial Hospital, Fort Erie, Ontario, 1963/1964.
Lennox and Addington Hospital, Napanee, Ontario, 1963/1966.
Parkwoods United Church, North York, Ontario, 1963/1964.
Peterborough Civic Hospital. Nurses Residence, Peterborough, Ontario, 1963/1964.
Prince of Wales Public School, Peterborough, Ontario, 1963/1965.
Queen Alexandra Public School, Peterborough, Ontario, 1963/1964.
Benmor Apartments, Peterborough, Ontario, 1963/1965.
Beth Israel Synagogue, Peterborough, Ontario, 1963/1964.
Burnview Apartments, Scarborough, Ontario, 1963/1964.
Edmison Heights Public School, Peterborough, Ontario, 1962/1963.
Ajax-Pickering General Hospital, Ajax, Ontario, 1961/1964.
Dare Residence, Kitchener, Ontario, 1961/1962.
Havelock District Public School, Havelock, Ontario, 1961/1963.
Peterborough District Composite School, Peterborough, Ontario, 1961/1964.
Kinsmen Garden Court Apartments, Peterborough, Ontario, 1960/1964.
Peterborough County Building, Peterborough, Ontario, 1959/1960.
St. Barnabus Anglican Church, Peterborough, Ontario, 1959/1960.
Kaufman House, Kitchener, Ontario, 1958/1959.
Peterborough Civic Hospital, Peterborough, Ontario, 1958/1960.
Peterborough Golf and Country Club, Peterborough, Ontario, 1958/1959.
Adam Scott Collegiate Vocational Institute, Peterborough, Ontario, 1958/1960.
Smith Farm House, Peterborough, Ontario, 1957/1957.
Cherney Residence, Peterborough, Ontario, 1957/1958.
Fairhaven Home for the Aged, Peterborough, Ontario, 1957/1960.
St. Margaret's United Church, Kingston, Ontario, 1956/1958.
West Ellesmere United Church, Scarborough, Ontario, 1956/1958.
Georgian Manor Home For The Aged, Penetanguishene, Ontario, 1955/1957.
Guelph General Hospital. Nurses Residence, Guelph, Ontario, 1955/1956.
Allemang House, Peterborough, Ontario, 1954/1955.
CHEX Radio Station, Peterborough, Ontario, 1954/1955.
Hamilton House, Peterborough, Ontario, 1954/1955.
Peterborough Coach House, Peterborough, Ontario, 1954/1954.
Peterborough Examiner Building, Peterborough, Ontario, 1954/1957.
Peterborough Medical Centre, Peterborough, Ontario, 1954/1957.
Peterborough Memorial Centre, Peterborough, Ontario, 1954/1955.
Grace United Church, Peterborough, Ontario, 1953/1954.
St. Giles Presbyterian Church, Peterborough, Ontario, 1953/1954.
St. John's Church Addition, Lakefield, Ontario, 1952/1953.

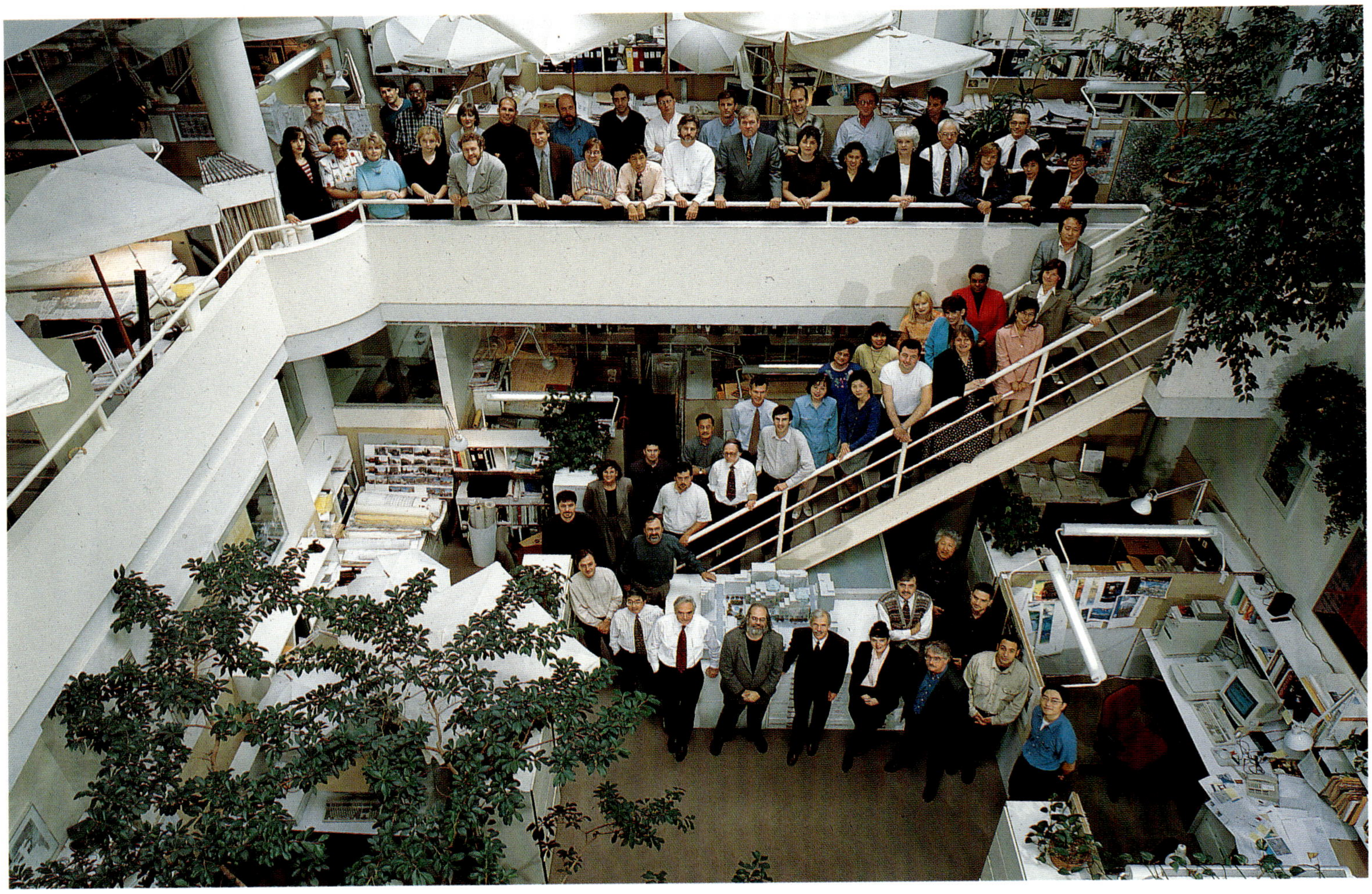

6861

Profile of Firm

One of North America's leading architectural firms, internationally-renowned for excellence in architectural design and urban planning, Zeidler Roberts Partnership/Architects developed from a practice that had its beginnings in 1880. The main office is located in Toronto with offices in West Palm Beach, Berlin, and London. The firm's professional and support staff is maintained at over one hundred members. The three senior partners are Eberhard Zeidler, Ian Grinnell and Peter Wakayama, and in addition, there are twenty-two partners and associates. The senior staff members have been with the firm for ten to thirty years.

Zeidler Roberts Partnership's experience includes not only numerous projects in Canada and the United States but also the United Kingdom, Germany, Spain, Russia, China, Hong Kong, Singapore, Thailand, Taiwan, Malaysia, Indonesia, Japan, the Caribbean, and Egypt.

Known for designing buildings which are innovative and successful, the firm has extensive experience in a wide variety of project types, including; retail, office, cultural, healthcare, residential, hotel, recreational, and institutional. Landmark projects include: The Toronto Eaton Centre (Toronto), Canada Place (Vancouver), Ontario Place (Toronto), The Gallery at Harborplace (Baltimore), Liberty Place - Phase II (Philadelphia), Raymond F. Kravis Centre for the Performing Arts (West Palm Beach), Queen's Quay Terminal (Toronto), Ford Centre for the Performing Arts (North York), The Hospital for Sick Children's Atrium patient tower (Toronto), Walter C. Mackenzie Health Sciences Centre (Edmonton), and MediaPark (Cologne, Germany).

The firm has received over one hundred national and international awards including five prestigious Governor General of Canada Medals for Architecture and four Massey Medals for Architecture (both awarded in conjunction with the Royal Architectural Institute of Canada).

Zeidler Roberts Partnership has established itself as a firm which combines award-winning design with great success in managing schedules and budgets. In addition to full architectural services, the firm also provides interior design, signage, master planning, feasibility studies, urban planning, systems development, and programming.

More than four hundred articles have been published on the firm's projects by leading professional magazines, including: "Architecture" (USA), "Progressive Architecture" (USA), "Architectural Record" (USA), "Architectural Review" (UK), "Architectural Design" (UK), "The Canadian Architect" (Canada), "Abitare" (Italy), "Domus" (Italy), "l'Arca" (Italy), "Bauen + Wohnen" (Switzerland), "L'Architecture d'Aujourd'hui" (France), "Process: Architecture" (Japan), "GA Documents" (Japan), "Space Design" (Japan) and "Nikkei Healthcare" (Japan) and "World Architecture" (UK).

The firm's work has also appeared in a number of architectural texts, such as *Architecture im Umbruch* by Jurgen Joedicke, *Structuralism in Architecture and Urban Planning* by Arnulf Luchinger, *Transformations in Modern Architecture* (Museum of Modern Art, New York) by Arthur Drexler, *Centres Commerciaux* by Patrick Mauger, *Hospital Interior Architecture* (Van Nostrand Reinhold, New York) by Jain Malkin, *Waterfronts: Cities Reclaim Their Edge* (McGraw-Hill, New York) by Ann Breen and Dick Rigby, and *The Journal of Canadian Art History*.

Mr. Zeidler has written two books: *Healing the Hospital* (Zeidler, 1974) recalls the innovative planning of McMaster University Health Sciences Centre and *Multi-Use Architecture in the Urban Context* (Kramer Verlag, 1983) has been published in four languages: English, German, French and Russian.

Eberhard Zeidler: In Search of Human Space (Ernst & Sohn, 1992) by Christian W. Thomsen, a 309 page monograph with over 700 illustrations, analyses Mr. Zeidler's career.